INVEST
TO
EMIGRATE

If you want to know how ...

Getting a Job in Australia

A step-by-step guide to finding work in Australia

Retire Abroad

Your complete guide to a new life in the sun

Living and Working in Australia

All you need to know for starting a new life 'down under'

Getting into Australia

The complete immigration guide to gaining your visa

Getting into America

The immigration guide to finding a new life in the USA

howtobooks

Please send for a free copy of the latest catalogue:

How To Books
3 Newtec Place, Magdalen Road,
Oxford OX4 1RE, United Kingdom
email: info@howtobooks.co.uk
http://www.howtobooks.co.uk

INVEST
TO
EMIGRATE

HOW TO GAIN PERMANENT RESIDENCE IN THE COUNTRY OF YOUR
CHOICE THROUGH INTERNATIONAL INVEST-TO-EMIGRATE PROGRAMMES

HENRY LIEBMAN

howtobooks

Published by How To Books Ltd,
3 Newtec Place, Magdalen Road,
Oxford OX4 1RE, United Kingdom.
Tel: (01865) 793806. Fax: (01865) 248780
Email: info@howtobooks.co.uk
www.howtobooks.co.uk

First edition 2005

British Library Cataloguing in Publication Data.
A catalogue record for this book is available from the
British Library

Cover design by Baseline Arts Ltd, Oxford
Produced for How To Books by Deer Park Productions,
Tavistock, Devon
Typeset by Pantek Arts Ltd, Maidstone, Kent
Printed and bound by Bell & Bain Ltd. Glasgow

Contents

Introduction

This book discusses the rules, pitfalls and advantages of the world's major immigrant investor programs; programs that offer permanent residence through a more or less passive investment. The process of researching the appropriate material led me to conclude that more countries offer immigrant investment programs than I could describe in a tome somewhat smaller than an encyclopedia. The emphasis here is on where people want to live, not tax havens. The most attention will be given to the most obvious programs: US, UK, Australia, New Zealand and Canada. We also include some of the lesser but still interesting locations frequently mentioned or sought by our clients, such as Switzerland, Costa Rica, Malta, Malaysia, Belize and Fiji. I have not included Greece because virtually all of the inbound immigration comes from EU countries whose nationals do not need to invest to obtain immigration status, and its immigration laws are still works in progress. Finally, I didn't convert currency because it's a moving target and because my currency seems to dwindle daily, making it too painful to do the research.

This book will help you choose a destination and give you some idea of whether you qualify or want to qualify for the particular program. Most countries, the most notable exception being the USA, offer straightforward investment options but give the examiner great discretion in determining the suitability of the applicant. Local assistance is very useful for overcoming an examiner's inate suspicions.

Once you choose a destination, you should contact a qualified attorney or migration consultant specializing in the particular program. In many instances, I solicited help from professionals focusing on a particular country. The truth of the matter is that there are very few people making their living by arranging immigration status for investors. There are even fewer qualified persons in the field. I asked those whose opinions I respect to contribute to this book. Please feel free to contact them directly.

I have practised US immigration law for some 20 years, specializing in visas pertaining to investors. While this doesn't make me an expert on immigrant investor programs world over, the US experience gives me a frame of reference and insights about the other programs I wouldn't otherwise have. I have attempted to ferret out each country's policies so that the reader can determine whether their goals fit with the host country goals. This is the first and most important step to making a successful application. Teaching pigs to dance always fails and irritates the pig.

Despite 9/11 and the West's conflict with radical Islam, more people these days travel for fun and immigrate for no other reason than a change of lifestyle than at any other time in history. Until the advent of jet transport, traveling for fun was a luxury reserved for the relatively rich. Before jet travel became affordable, travel took too long and cost too much. According to the World Tourism Organization, over 700 million people took a trip for pleasure in 2003. About 56% went to Europe, 16% to the Americas, and 18% to Asia Pacific countries.

Most immigration for lifestyle is to the English speaking world from the rest of the world. The USA, alone, accepts approximately 1,000,000 permanent residents per year. Additionally, several million illegal immigrants, mostly from Mexico and Central America, with a greater number of Canadians than one might think, live in the US on a permanent basis. It's difficult to obtain a firm number because estimates may or may not include dependents of the principal applicant. Also the fact that a visa was issued does not necessarily mean that the recipient of the visa actually landed as a permanent resident. In the case of the USA, recording comings and goings of immigrants was not of paramount importance until after 9/11. Recall that two of the 9/11 hijackers' student visas for pilot training were approved after the event.

The EU countries also accept large numbers of immigrants, for different reasons. EU nationals are not restricted from living and working in other EU countries. Refugees or simply illegals from the Asian land mass, home to most of the world's population, may use land transport to cross porous borders rather than arrive by boat or plane at a port or airport policed by customs and immigration officials. By any estimation, a lot of people are on the move for a lot of reasons.

Immigration past and present

Movement of peoples is fundamental to human history. Neanderthal man wandered for food. Neolithic man learned to use tools to produce food rather than wander when food supplies dwindled. The advent of cities and towns caused townspeople to trade, colonize and import goods and skills to supplement local resources that no longer supported the population.

For most of history, immigration in the modern sense was impossible. One had to be born to the land in order to obtain full rights. All visitors, regardless of period of stay, were sojourners. Of course there were exceptions such as marrying in, buying in or making an extraordinary contribution. The general rule prevented anything like the immigration patterns we know today.

Until the advent of the information age, most organized immigration consisted of slavery, and corvée (or forced) labor. Nomads and refugees always did and will continue to exist. In the case of corvée or state sponsored immigration, the king simply rounded up folks and put them to work. Corvée labor still exists. Stalin and Mao Tse Tung, as Nebuchadnezzar before them, removed entire populations for strategic and economic reasons. The classical Greeks refined slavery to a highly regulated system of property rights that existed until the 1860s in Russia and the USA. The principle difference between slavery and corvée labor is that corvée labor theoretically has an end to it. By the 1860s, slavery was banned in most places and replaced by indentured servitude.

Australia was originally settled by transported convicts and then by indentured servants. The northern states of the USA relied on indentured servitude for labor, while the southern states relied upon slavery. Canada and New Zealand were more middle-class enterprises.

Immigration, as we know it today, derives from the industrial and, more particularly, the information revolutions. The industrial revolution began to shrink time and space. The first immigration wave from Europe to North America, Australia, parts of South America and South Africa occurred in the late 1800s up to the 1920s. This immigration wave stemmed from the host countries' desire to populate new lands with Europeans. As the host countries' appetites for new population were satisfied, legal barriers to immigration became the norm.

Between 1900 and 2000, humankind went from traveling by sailing boat and horse, to traveling at multiples of the speed of sound, not to mention reaching the moon. Information went from reading about the travels of Marco Polo or Captain Cook several years after the event, to watching world events unfold in real time on satellite television.

The management of exponentially increased information flows required complex systems and greater specialization of labor for maintenance, storage, and dissemination of information. Operating at real time requires greater flexibility to deal with ever-changing circumstances. This, in turn, requires still greater specialization of skills. By the mid-1970s, international employers began to comb the world for the specialized skills required to service this complex infrastructure. This started a new wave of immigration that continues today, only slightly reduced by the impacts of 9/11.

As strange as this may sound, the world's larger inbound markets reacted by removing barriers to immigration. In historical terms, immigration is easier, not harder, than before. For example, the USA finally got around to repealing the Asian Exclusion Act in 1976. It's hard to believe that prior to 1976 Asians, except for Japanese under the so called 'Gentlemens' Agreement', were categorically excluded from the USA. The EU formed in part as a reaction to globalization. Europe required a larger market, with fewer barriers to trade and people's movements, to compete for skills in the ever-shrinking world. In this context, globalization refers to the need to integrate skills from all parts of the world to support real time complex systems.

This is not to say that all road blocks to immigration vanished. Every time a country liberalizes immigration, there's an influx. The influx reaches a point where it coincides with an economic downturn, causing local labor and local chauvinists to complain and politicians to tighten the rules. The return of good times increases demand for skills and a consequential liberalization of the immigration rules.

The UK offers a case in point. Under Tony Blair, the UK implemented what are probably the most liberal immigration policies in the world to attract skilled workers and entrepreneurs. Now that the bloom is off the boom, we'll see how long those policies last.

The same globalization trends make investment immigration, or immigration for lifestyle reasons rather than employment, possible. The major inbound countries – US, UK, Australia, New Zealand and Canada – as well as a host of other countries, devised immigrant investment schemes as a way to attract capital and entrepreneurial skills.

While the investment schemes vary and ebb and flow in relation to the economic climate, the goal is to attract business-savvy immigrants with capital who will foster economic growth as a by-product of their investment in the host country. During good times, the critics complain of immigrants buying a visa. How unfair, my grandparents floated here on a three-month voyage on a rotten ship while the modern fat cats arrive in first class. This chorus empowers the authorities, who don't need prompting, to tighten the program and restrict entry. In bad times, local governments complain of tax revenue shortfalls and unemployment. All of a sudden immigrant investors no longer buy immigration status, but become legitimate sources of capital and out comes the red carpet.

The UK, US and New Zealand offer private sector managed programs. Canada and Australia nationalized their programs in response to abuses that occurred during the boom times of the mid to late 90s. The US, whose program was born out of the 1990 recession, unilaterally froze its program in 1998 only to dust it off again in 2003 in response to the recession. The UK amended its program in 2004 because it was so expensive that very few people applied.

As a general rule, investor capital is much safer with the nationalized Australian and Canadian programs. The privately managed programs offer greater flexibility and greater variety of investment options.

Ours is the first generation in human history where hundreds of millions of people travel for fun, work abroad primarily for the experience, or simply pull up stakes and move to a nicer clime. When was the last time humankind strung two generations of wealth together without a major wealth-destroying conflagration? Virtually any freeholder in Western Europe, Japan or Korea can sell the family home, or use an inheritance, to relocate to Australia, North America and a host of other countries simply by making a passive investment.

Let's investigate the options!

1 · Australia

The geography of Australia may be succinctly described as a giant South Pacific island with large deserts in the middle. Australia's landmass, while larger than the USA, contains approximately 16 million people, compared to approximately 280 million people in the USA, and over 600 million people in Western Europe. One could say Australia is basically empty.

The coasts of Australia generally have temperate climates without excessive heat and with little or no snow. In the tropical north-east, the state of Queensland offers year-round warm weather and fantastic beaches. Most of the population live between Melbourne and Sydney. Perth on the west coast fronting the Indian ocean is the other population center. Australian cities tend to be clean, well-kept and user-friendly. In short, Australia offers a superior quality of life in terms of the quality of food, living space, housing and creature comforts in general.

Australia is a member of the British Commonwealth, subject to the over-riding power of the Queen of England's Governor General. The Governor General rarely interferes in local politics but does have the power to dissolve Parliament and call new elections. This is the case in any Commonwealth country. The States of Australia have their own parliaments, usually with upper and lower houses. The federal government is also based on a parliamentary system.

Australians, from time to time, debate withdrawing from the Commonwealth and becoming a republic like the USA. The debate generally stems from the Whitlam affair when in 1975 the Governor General dissolved Parliament and essentially deposed the elected Prime Minister, Gough Whitlam; more on this later. Australia offers government-funded pension and health benefits that vary in each state. Australians view themselves as middle-class without great disparity between rich and poor. Visitors will find most Australians out-going and friendly.

While the government encourages immigration, the immigration programs are strictly managed and the subject of intense public debate. Quotas and the acceptable categories of investors and skilled workers tend to change in accordance with the political tides. Australia will probably maintain a relatively aggressive immigration policy for years to come; if for no other reason than to create a critical mass of population to maintain a continental economy. Whether a healthy economy depends on ever-expanding population is a question open to debate.

History

It is generally accepted that the first humans traveled across the sea to Australia from Indonesia about 70,000 years ago. According to Gavin Menzies, author of *1421 the year China Discovered America*, there is evidence that Chinese voyages of discovery reached Australia in or about the year 1422. I highly recommend this book to those who enjoy creative and thought-provoking thinking. This is a gratuitous plug because I've never met Mr. Menzies. Europeans, utilizing maps dating from the Chinese voyages, reached Australia in the 16th century. The Portuguese were followed by the Dutch and then followed by the English pirate William Dampier.

Colonization by the British

Captain James Cook reached the east coast in 1770, landing at Botany Bay. Cook claimed the continent for the British and named it New South Wales. Australia, then known as Terra Incognita, or 'unknown land', was being marketed in London to unsuspecting migrants prior to Captain Cook's arrival. The fact is that the British Admiralty was certain Australia existed due to sailors' reports and because it was marked on Dutch, Portuguese and Venetian maps.

The British were also competing with French and Spanish voyage of discovery fleets to claim the continent. Evidently Cook had secret orders to proceed to Australia and he successfully eluded and beat the rival explorers to the punch.

Settlement by convicts

British interest in Australia was spurred by loss of the penal colony of Georgia to the newly formed United States of America. The expense of colonizing Australia was said to not be worth the reward but for the penal colony problem. In 1787, the First Fleet set sail for Botany Bay under the command of Captain Arthur Philip, the first governor. The first fleet included 11 ships, 750 male and female convicts, four companies of marines and supplies for two years. Philip first arrived in Botany Bay on 26 January 1788, but moved north to Sydney Cove, where he found fresh water and higher land. Most of the first fleet settlers perished more from maltreatment than from starvation. Remember, victors write history so starvation is the party line. Several succeeding fleets were required to secure the Sydney Cove colony.

The penal colony past created a culture that prizes 'mateship', i.e. equality and mutual assistance as well as entrepreneurship. These two qualities underpin Australian culture today. During World War II the Australians who were interned in Japanese prison camps, which were horrible, acted more or less as a tribe and had higher survival rates than the Americans, British or Dutch.

Gold, farming and mining

The dry and largely uninhabitable interior prevented colonization of the entire continent. As a result the bulk of the population lives in the coastal cities of Sydney, Melbourne, Perth and Brisbane. In the 1850s non-convict settlers came to prospect for gold in the areas to the north of Melbourne. The influx of settlers resulted in increased farming and mineral extraction as well as the destruction of the aboriginal populations. Mineral extraction, wool and wheat continue to play a major role in the Australian economy.

Australia in the 20th century

Australia converted from a federation of the separate colonies to a country and a member of the commonwealth on 1 January 1901. The nation joined the British and later the USA in most of the wars of the 20th century including World War II and the various wars against communist states. In World War II the Japanese bombed Port Moresby, Darwin and Broome in the north. Things were so desperate that the British, arguably without the knowledge of many Australians, planned to retreat to defensive positions defending Sydney and the south against a Japanese invasion. Many Australians continue to feel a sense of betrayal. The Australians were the first to stem the Japanese tide by defeating them at Milne Bay in New Guinea. After the US success in the Battle of the

Coral Sea, Australian troops joined the USA in pushing the Japanese out of the Pacific islands.

After World War II Australia embarked on a campaign to fill the country with immigrants. Australian immigration rules always promoted immigration of those with trades, higher education or the willingness to start a business. The variable, which ebbs and flows according to the political winds, is race under the guise of language. There have been a few periods when Asians could easily migrate to Australia. At some point race and language become an issue and the points allocated to English language ability become more important, thus restricting immigration to English speakers. Today Australia is a land of immigrants. The majority are of English or European origin, with significant Asian and other Muslim communities.

The Gough Whitlam affair

Every Australian knows of the Gough Whitlam affair. If you plan to move to Australia you should know the basic facts also. The Vietnam era unrest saw the election of the Labor government headed by Gough Whitlam. The Whitlam government withdrew Australian troops from Vietnam, abolished national service and higher education fees, instituted a system of free and universally available health care, and supported land rights for Aboriginal people. At the time this was radical stuff bordering on communism.

On 11 November 1975, the governor general (the Queen's representative in Australia) dismissed Parliament and installed Malcolm Fraser, of the opposition Liberal Party, as prime minister. The rumor at the time was that Whitlam was in league with the communists, causing the British, urged on by the US CIA, to stage a coup to prevent a left-wing take-over. During those years the CIA was thought to be deeply involved in the coup business so there could be some truth to the rumor. The vast majority of the population, regardless of political persuasion, was shocked the governor general exercised what was thought to be an obsolete and undemocratic vestige of royal authority. The irony of this interference in Australian affairs is that it was more than likely unnecessary. Whitlam's Labor party was loosing popularity and probably would have lost the next election scheduled a few months later.

The Republic of Australia?

The proposal of becoming a republic, which entails replacing the British monarch with an Australian head of state, was put to a vote in 1999. While it is thought that the majority of Australians favored becoming a republic, the question on the 1999 ballot was intertwined with other unpopular issues and failed. Given the appropriate political climate this issue will probably reappear.

Immigrant investors

The Australian program, due to its price, not nearly as popular as the Canadian program, has managed to attract AU $187 million since its inception in 1995. Australia, like Canada, nationalized its program in response to abuses of the rules and numerous cases of the hoodwinking of unsuspecting immigrants. Generally, the Australian program requires an investment of AU$750,000 to AU$2 million in a designated state bond. The state uses the funds to pay for services and infrastructure.

This program requires wealth and skills. Applicants must have accumulated the qualifying assets entirely through their own efforts. This means gifts and inheritances generally don't count. While the investment program waives the normal requirement of establishing a business within three years of landing, applicants must undertake to go into a business or other self-employment in an undefined 'medium term'.

Australia offers two investment tracks: independent and state sponsored. The Australian rules are purposefully subjective and allow the examiners great latitude in assessing an applicant's eligibility. In addition each state of Australia has its own subjective requirements for sponsorship. For these reasons, our discussion will focus on policy rather than the detail of the rules.

Independent investors

Independent investors must maintain their designated investment of AU$1,500,000 for four years and be under 45 years of age. Designated investments are generally bonds issued by a state of Australia. Very few people use this category because of the age requirement and the high investment amount. Not many 45 year olds have AU$1,500,000, particularly at current exchange rates.

Independent investors receive a provisional visa, valid for four years. To transfer to permanent status, the investor must make a further application showing that the investment was maintained, the applicant lived in Australia for two of the four years, and that the applicant has a real and demonstrable commitment to establishing a business or investments in Australia.

General requirements

The general requirements for the provisional visa are:

- You have an overall successful record of business or investment activities with a demonstrable high level of management skills.

- You have a total of at least three years' experience in actively managing a qualifying business(es) or investment(s).

- In one of the past five fiscal years, you have continually directed a business with at least 10% ownership interest or directly managed eligible investments of at least AU$1,500,000.

- For the two fiscal years immediately preceding your application, your (and your spouse/partner's) net assets were worth at least $2,250,000.

- At the time of decision, you have made a designated investment of not less than AU$1,500,000 (amount to be determined by the points test).

- You have not been involved in business or investment activities considered unacceptable in Australia.

- You have a genuine commitment to maintain business or investment activity in Australia after the designated investment matures.

- You are able to meet strict health standards and provide evidence that you are of good character.

- You speak vocational English.

- You are 45 years of age or younger.

To sum it up, English-speaking successful business people under 45 with the intent to do business in Australia may qualify.

State sponsored visas

State sponsored visas offer a way around the language and age requirements. Simply put, applicants must first approach the state government
for sponsorship. Each state has different rules. Western Australia and
Queensland have been very proactive in attracting investors.

As in the case of independent investors, sponsored investors receive a
provisional visa valid for four years. Provisional status will be waived if
the applicant maintained the investment for four years, and was resident
in the sponsoring state or territory for two years of the four-year period.

To qualify for Western Australian sponsorship, business applicants must
submit a business plan or demonstrate exceptional business skills. To
locate within a 50km radius of the Perth central business district, one
must also produce a plan that convinces the state authorities that it will
generate employment, develop export markets, replace imports or
introduce new skills or technologies. The rules state that investor applicants only need to show compliance with the minimum federal
requirements. The truth is somewhere in between. The State of Western
Australia obviously wants skills and capital. The more you have of both,
the easier it is.

Basic requirements

Once one obtains state sponsorship the basic requirements are:

● You have an overall successful record of business or investment activities.

● You have a total of at least three years' experience in actively managing a qualifying business(es) or investment(s).

● In one of the past five fiscal years, you have continually directed a
business with at least 10% ownership interest or managed eligible
investments of at least AU$750,000.

● For the two fiscal years immediately preceding your application,
your (and your spouse/partner's) net assets were worth at least
AU$1,125,000.

● At the time of decision, you have made a designated investment of
not less than AU$750,000.

- You have not been involved in business or investment activities considered unacceptable in Australia.

- You have a genuine commitment to maintain business or investment activity in Australia after the designated investment matures.

- You are able to meet strict health standards and provide evidence that you are of good character.

- You are 55 years of age or younger at the time of application or the state has waived the age requirement due to exceptional economic benefit to the state.

Conclusion

All investors must also qualify under the points system. The important points concern age, education and language. To some degree, increasing the investment amount and/or receiving state sponsorship may overcome non-qualifying scores.

Australia's is among the more thorough and efficient immigration systems in the world. That doesn't mean they process petitions quickly; it simply means they are meticulous. While the concept of purchasing a state bond sounds simple enough, state sponsorship is not always easily obtained and the requirement that one must undertake to engage in some sort of investment activity after the provisional period gives the government a way to revoke petitions. Revocation of the visa for failure to engage in an investment activity is rare but it is a theoretical possibility.

Australian states don't pay finder's fees or commissions nor are there schemes such as in Canada to finance the investment capital. This means nobody pushes the investment category, except possibly the state governments. Government being what it is, that means nobody pushes the investor program. Hence the investor and immigration consultant must battle the beauracracy without local allies. On the other hand, Australia offers great lifestyle, standard of living and weather, as well as decent medical care and pensions. The hassle might be worth it.

Mathew Collins and Frans Buysse contributed to this article. Frans Buysse has been active in the field of migration since 1986. He started working as a consultant for the Dutch Emigration Centres and later became immigration officer for the Canadian Embassy. In 1993, he founded Buysse Immigration Consultancy, a team of professional consultants offering a full package of services to prospective immigrants to Australia, Canada, New Zealand and the United States of America.

Email: buysse@visaspecialist.com

Mathew Collins is founder of Ambler Collins, one of Europe's oldest multi-destinational immigration consultancies. Ambler Collins maintains branch offices in London, Sydney and the USA.

Email: Mathew@amblercollins.com

2 · Belize

Belize, formerly British Honduras, is located in Central America on the Caribbean Sea and offers tropical living in an English-speaking country. The lack of modern roads and infrastructure makes life slow and laid back. Belize is a parliamentary democracy that, unlike most of its neighbors, has been coup free. Tourists and residents alike enjoy some of the best diving in the world, fantastic beaches, Mayan ruins, virgin jungle, and an ample array of eco-lodges. Medical care and housing can be found at very reasonable costs and at European or North American standards.

Retirees and other immigrants

Belize targets British, Canadian and US retirees. Aside from cheap living and beautiful beaches, Belize offers favorable tax treatment. Belize does not tax retirees on income brought into Belize from abroad or earned abroad and left abroad. Belize only taxes income earned in Belize. Retirees may not work in Belize without a work permit but may form companies that direct foreign business activities or their own affairs without paying Belize tax or violating the ban on working in Belize. Many people base themselves in Belize for tax reasons and do business elsewhere. This is easy to accomplish because Belize has no minimum residency period to retain immigration status.

If you want a second passport, you should consider carefully before deciding on Belize unless you want to live there anyway. There have been several passport scandals, which have caused many countries to not recognize a Belize passport for tax purposes, or, in some cases, as an entry document.

Permanent residence

One may apply for permanent residence after one year continuous legal residence in Belize, by paying the permanent residence fee of US$100, and an additional amount ranging from US$100 to US$1,200 depending on the nationality of the applicant. This deposit may be refunded three years after residency is granted. Permanent residents may work in Belize but are taxed in Belize. They may apply for citizenship after five years of continuous permanent residence.

For most people, the fastest and easiest way to move to Belize is through the retirement program managed by the Ministry of Tourism. Retirees may apply immediately, without waiting a year, as in the case of permanent residents.

The retirement program

The rules, as immigration rules go, are straightforward. To qualify, the principal applicant must be 45 years of age or older and have a monthly income stream of at least US$2,000 per month generated overseas. At least US$2,000 per month must be remitted to a Belize financial institution. Spouses and dependent children automatically qualify. Applicants must provide proof that the source of the pension is reliable and that the applicant is entitled to the pension. The exact standards for proving a secure source of funds change from time to time. At the moment, the institution providing the pension must certify it has been in existence 20 years or more, that the applicant is entitled to the pension of US$2,000 per month, and a chartered accountant must certify the same. The applicant must also provide two bank references. The requirements are relaxed when the pension comes from a Fortune 500 company or the like.

Duty-free imports

Retirees receive a one-time allowance to import a car and personal and household effects duty-free. Thereafter, there are provisions for importing personal effects, boats, planes and cars tax-free. Obviously, the authorities will look for abuses of the rules, such as the importation of goods beyond what one household could reasonably use.

Conclusion

To conclude, residency and tax benefits may be quickly had and at very reasonable costs. The rules change with rapidity, which is why we only offer a brief outline. Most people use Belize as a second home or tax home. The minority of foreigners who actually live in Belize can enjoy a tropical lifestyle without much of the hassle of a third world country.

3 · Bermuda

This chapter is short because the rules are simple and clear. Bermuda is a crowded and sought after location. There are less than 300 homes for sale and they are expensive. The laws are designed to encourage visitors and discourage immigration.

Overview

Bermuda consists of six main islands encompassing less than 21 square miles. The islands are the top of a seamount and enjoy a temperate climate with beaches, golf and water sport activities. Due to favorable tax laws, Bermuda is a favored destination for offshore companies, particularly insurance companies. The islands are a popular tourist destination as well as home to a small and select group of wealthy families and individuals.

History

The first recorded visitor, Juan de Bermudez, was shipwrecked on Bermuda's reefs in 1503. Over the years, mariners from most of the seafaring nations of Western Europe were shipwrecked on Bermuda reefs. Bermuda's first settlers came in 1609 when the *Sea Venture* of the British Third Supply Fleet was wrecked on a reef on its way to Virginia. Soon settlers started coming to Bermuda on purpose. Bermuda became a British crown colony in 1684.

Government

Bermuda is a self-governing overseas territory of the United Kingdom. It makes its own local laws that apply equally to everyone regardless of nationality. The territory has a parliamentary system of government. Although the British Queen, acting through her appointed Governor General, is the official head of state, all laws are made and executed in Bermuda. There is also a Bermuda Society, formed in 1987 and composed primarily of prominent overseas Bermudians, that promotes Bermuda's image, trade and cultural interests throughout the world.

Immigration policy

Because Bermuda is a small densely-populated island, immigration and land ownership laws are very strict. The policy is to prevent speculative real estate development and to make sure the vast majority of the housing stock is available to Bermudans. Some 64,000 people live on the islands of Bermuda.

As a general rule, foreigners simply cannot buy undeveloped land. Non-Bermudians may buy residences only if the house has an annual rental value (a formula used to calculate land tax) of US$126,000 or greater. This means that only the highest priced properties are available to non-Bermudians. The annual rental value is adjusted, mostly up, from time to time. The current housing stock available to foreigners is less than 300 homes, with prices starting at approximately US$2,000,000. Buying a condominium or strata title development is permitted in designated developments where the unit value exceeds approximately US$650,000.

To further inhibit speculation, non-Bermudians may only own one house at one time. In certain cases, second properties may be purchased, but only on the condition that the original property is sold within 12 months.

On top of the already high housing prices, one must obtain a license from the Ministry of Labor and Home Affairs. An application fee of currently $1,152.00 must be paid upon submitting the form. The fee is refunded upon approval. At that time, you pay the real fee, which is 22% of the purchase price for a house or 15% of the purchase price for a condominium. In other words, add 22% to the purchase price of a house in Bermuda.

Foreigners who own houses in Bermuda generally come for a period of several months or less. It's relatively easy to stay for six months or less if you can prove you maintain primary ties abroad. Persons who own the freehold or have a lease of 25 years or more may apply for a residence permit valid for one year. Residence permit holders must agree not to seek employment, prove they are financially self-sufficient, and prove they maintain primary ties abroad.

It's very difficult to work on Bermuda. Work permits are based on proof that the skills are unavailable in Bermuda. These laws are strictly enforced and permits are only issued for a year. It's nearly impossible to obtain permanent residence unless you are a long-term resident of say 20 years or more, or have close family in Bermuda. I say it's nearly impossible because while I couldn't find a law authorizing long-term residence to foreigners with no ties to Bermuda. I refuse to give up and say it's impossible. On the other hand, with less than 300 homes available and the bulk of those taken by temporary visitors, obtaining long-term residency may be an impossible task.

Conclusion

The laws of Bermuda discourage property ownership by foreigners and immigration. The message is that they welcome visitors but not residents. Given the land shortage and the population density, about 3,100 people per square mile, I can understand the government's reasoning.

4 · Canada

Canada may be best described as 'vast'. Virtually all of the population, some 30 million, lives on a 4,000-mile-long, 100-mile-deep strand along Canada's southern border with the USA. This is probably the world's largest undefended border. The rest of the country, which continues north to the polar ice cap, is sparsely populated at best. The climate ranges from the cold winters and muggy summers of the eastern part of the country, to the cool maritime climate of the West. Victoria, located on the southern tip of Vancouver Island, and the capital of the Province of British Columbia, offers the most temperate climate in the country.

The scenery is for the most part stunning. Anybody who enjoys outdoor activities would be at home in Canada, with its world class fishing, climbing, hiking, and skiing. Probably the biggest cultural difference between the USA and Canada is that Canada encourages maintenance of ethnic traditions whereas the USA encourages its citizens to join the melting pot and become whatever the USA has or will become. Canada both politically and culturally welcomes immigrants.

The Canadian system of government and the country's social norms offer a 'European alternative' to the more unabashed capitalism of the USA. Canada has a parliamentary system more similar to the system in the UK than to the US federal system. Canada is a confederation of provinces rather than a federal republic. In practical terms this means that Canadian provinces have the theoretical right to secede and generally have more power to regulate external affairs than US states. Having said this, Quebec's strong separatist political party has yet to test the system. Canada remains part of the British Commonwealth.

Canada's publicly funded medical and pension benefits compare with those of Western Europe. The European-style social benefits come with the resultant high levels of taxation. While Canadians tend to be better educated and probably a bit more cultured than their neighbors to the south, the much smaller domestic market coupled with higher taxation mean it is arguably more difficult to make a buck. The Canadian dollar is freely exchangeable and for the last 10 years at least, has been worth less than its US counterpart.

NAFTA, the North American Free Trade Agreement, aims for integration of the US, Canadian and Mexican markets. The reality is something different. Canadian and US investors and skilled workers, generally professional workers, may come to work in either country if they have pre-arranged employment. NAFTA privileges apply to citizens, not permanent residents or non-immigrants. NAFTA reduced tariffs on many items but several exceptions still exist.

The Canadian-US border, while undefended, unlike European borders, still requires inspections. Border crossing lines at busy crossings such as the crossings serving Vancouver B.C., Toronto and Montreal can be quite long and frustrating.

History

By 1000 AD, the Vikings, the first European visitors, tried to settle northern Newfoundland and failed. Although a number of European countries were interested in establishing settlements in the Americas, the French explorer Jacques Cartier made the first claim on the area surrounding the St Lawrence River in 1534. The Europeans found a large variety of Indian tribes occupying most of the land. At first the Indians were accommodating, but soon turned hostile as European settlement and encroachment on Indian lands increased.

Settlement by the French

By 1663 Canada, with a population of about 3000 French settlers mostly living on the fur trade, became a province of France. The British soon followed, founding the Hudson's Bay Company in 1670. As in most French and British cohabitations until modern times, war ensued. In short, the British and French came to blows in Europe, with the conflict spreading to Canada, culminating in the Seven Years War and the British victory by General Wolf over General Montcalm at the Plains of Abraham before Quebec City. The Treaty of Paris in 1763 resulted in the French handover of Canada to Britain.

This conflict sowed the seeds of the current separatist issues between the French-speaking Province of Quebec and the rest of the country, which is English speaking. Canada is a confederation of provinces, not a federal republic like the USA. The Canadian High Court has ruled that a province may secede under certain conditions.

Migration and war

During the American Revolution (1776–83), about 50,000 'Loyalists' from the USA moved to Canada, adding to the English-speaking population. The migration of Loyalists continued through the War of 1812 between the USA and Britain. The war of 1812, ostensibly about preventing the USA from trading with Napoleonic France, was a disguised attempt to win back the US colonies. Canada fought on the British side. The USA attempted to invade Canada to no avail.

At the time of the US Civil War (1860–65) the USA was much more populous and industrialized than Canada. By the end of the Civil War the US army was among the most powerful armies in the world and without a mission. At the same time the USA rewarded many war veterans with soldiers' scrip that could be used to purchase federal lands in the West. Many settlers found their way to Canada also. The British, fearful of losing Canada to a Union Army with time on its hands, instituted the British North America Act (BNA Act) in 1867. The Act established the Dominion of Canada and became Canada's equivalent of a constitution. This Act was soon followed by the construction of a transcontinental railway, designed to tie the Canadian provinces together, which was completed in 1885. By 1912 all the provinces joined the confederation except Newfoundland, which finally joined in 1949.

Immigration from Europe

Between dominion and World War II, Canada recruited immigrants primarily from Europe. The settlement patterns mirrored those of the USA. Generally speaking, the majority of settlers in this period were Irish, then Italian and then Eastern European, Jewish and Slavic. There were many scams whereby Jews from Eastern Europe bought cheap passage to the USA only to find themselves in Montreal, where they mostly remained. Most settlers tend to pick places that resemble home. For example, many Eastern European immigrants settled the Canadian plains, focusing in Saskatchewan, Alberta and Manitoba. Winnipeg to this day has a large Eastern European community.

After World War II, Canada purposefully recruited immigrants, again, primarily from Europe. The Canadian government uses immigration to settle the country and enlarge the domestic market; the theory being that the population needs to reach a certain size to support a continental economy. To that end the authorities set annual targets and send officials to recruit in particular markets. For example, the Canadian government attracted significant Hong Kong capital, primarily to Vancouver, during the years preceding the handover of Hong Kong to the Chinese. There were also concerted attempts to attract Scots, Dutch farmers and Hungarians during the 1956 revolt; it's a long list. During the 1990s immigrants started coming from the Middle East, Caribbean islands, Pakistan and India.   All major Canadian cities include significant Indian and Pakistani communities.

Recent history

Immigration played a great role in Canada's postwar economic expansion and prosperity. Even with continuing large immigration levels, particularly as a percentage of population, Canada is a primarily urban society living in a long thin band along the US border.

In 1975 Canada largely settled native land claims by granting mineral royalties and some control over vast swathes of the northern portion of the country.

The ever-increasing numbers of non-French and, for that matter, non-English-speaking immigrants to Montreal and, to a lesser degree Quebec City, may have been the spark that caused the most recent rise of the Parti Quebecois, which barely lost a vote to secede from Canada in 1995. The current situation could be summed up by concluding that Quebec can't afford to leave the confederation even if the majority desired to do so. Quebec currently enjoys many benefits by being treated as a 'distinct society'. The English-speaking provinces largely don't care if Quebec leaves. Naturally those who rule would rather rule over more than less, and the USA would not welcome a new country on the continent, simply on the grounds that things work well they way they are and there's no point risking the current peaceful situation. The tea leaves seem to point to a maintenance of the status quo for the foreseeable future.

One challenge to Canada for the new century is how to maintain a European-style social safety net with the consequent high taxes when they live next to the USA which is going in the other direction. The

European Community countries provide a much more similar level of social services than do the USA and Canada. This disparity creates a significant issue of Canadians and their capital flowing south to take advantage of US economic opportunity and lower taxes, while utilizing the Canadian social safety net without paying for it.

The other challenge is the integration of a large and continually growing immigrant population. Canada's drive to create population critical mass continues. Virtually every economic growth theory assumes population growth. One would think that at some point humankind will need to make more with less. In any event the immigrant issue is more talk than real. The North American experience has been that virtually every immigrant group has assimilated smoothly into the overall culture over two to three generations. All in all Canada has been a successful economic and social story, in that large waves of disparate immigrant groups have been woven into a cohesive society with a high level of civil rights and a prosperous economy.

Immigrant investment

Canada offers the most established and the most widely used passive immigrant investment program in the world. Canada accepts close to 2,000 immigrant investor applicants annually. Under the Canadian model, investor immigrants can enjoy the benefits of a national healthcare program, affordable first class education and a national pension system that provides measurable annual income upon retirement.

The Canadian confederation

The British established Canada as a confederation of previously independent provinces and territories in 1867. Confederations occur for negative reasons. Nobody gives up independence out of choice. In this case, the negative reason was protection against a feared invasion from the US. The Union army, victorious in the US civil war, was the largest and most modern army in the world at the time, with nothing to do but tame the west and the rest of the continent if it was so decided. The British formed the Canadian confederation and built a transcontinental railroad just in case.

Two systems

The fact that Canada is a confederation is important to investment immigration because provinces have more rights than states in a federal system. In the Canadian context, this plays out through what amounts to a dual immigration system. Investors can therefore choose between a federal program offered by the English-speaking provinces, and a more popular program exclusively managed by French-speaking Quebec. The Quebec program offers significantly faster processing times.

Through the 1980s and most of the 90s, Canada's investment immigration program entailed a private sector investment. As a result of real and perceived abuses of the program, the Canadian government nationalized its investor program. Quebec, being semi-independent anyway, provincialized its program. Both programs now provide investors with government guarantees for the return of capital.

The federal investor program

The investment capital

The federal investor program requires an investment of CD$400,000, which is deposited with the Receiver General of Canada, and a personal net worth of CD$800,000 with business experience. The investment delivers no interest and must be maintained for five years. Applicants may state a desire to live anywhere in Canada except Quebec. The investment is government guaranteed and the proceeds are allocated to the provinces excluding Quebec.

Investor qualifications

Canada wishes to attract business acumen and investment capital. A qualified applicant typically owns or manages an active trade or business, which may include professional practices, rather than merely managing investment activities. In this context, gray areas include professionals who don't manage the business, passive real estate investors and investment managers. For example, developing real estate may qualify, whereas merely owning real estate may not. Gifts and inheritances only qualify where the applicant parlayed the gift or inheritance into a business that they actively manage.

The regulations attempt to define the scale of the required management experience. Management experience must include direction of an enterprise with five or more full-time employees or compliance with two of four 'bright light' tests. The regulations examine two years within the period beginning five years before the date of the application and ending on the day of application denial or approval. They include the following stipulations:

- Percentage of ownership in the enterprise times number of full-time employees – not less than two

- Percentage of ownership times total annual sales – not less than CD$500,000

- Percentage of ownership times net income – not less than CD$50,000

- Percentage of ownership times year end net assets – not less than CD$125,000

Financing the investment

The federal program permits applicants to finance their investment through designated banking institutions. Typically, the financing schemes require a down payment of CD$120,000. The bank loans the applicant the balance of CD$280,000. The applicant deposits the sum of CD$400,000 with the Receiver General. The Canadian government guarantees repayment of the bank loan, not the investor's down payment.

The bank takes fees and interest from the down payment, and the immigration agent takes their commissions from the down payment. The federal government disburses the net proceeds to the provinces for use in a variety of public projects. The investor forfeits the down payment, so the net cost of the transaction to the investor is the down payment. The five-year investment period begins following visa issuance.

The Quebec immigrant investor program

The Quebec program is virtually the same as the federal program, with the following important distinctions:

- The investment is guaranteed by the Province of Quebec

- Professionals such as doctors, dentists, accountants and lawyers do not qualify for management experience

- One must state an intention to settle in Quebec

- The investment proceeds are allocated to the Province of Quebec rather than the English-speaking provinces

- The five-year investment period begins following Quebec approval, even before the investor comes to Canada

If the investor is refused by the federal authorities for a medical or security inadmissibility, the investment is refunded.

One may finance the investment in a manner similar to the federal program except that the Province of Quebec designates securities brokerage firms and investment institutions to finance the investment rather than banks.

The Quebec program has been more popular than the Federal program because processing is faster and they pay brokers higher commissions. It's that simple. The final result is no different from the federal program except that an applicant must land in the Province of Quebec. But the Canadian constitution allows Canadian permanent residents to land in Quebec and move elsewhere later.

Some useful hints

There is no advantage in investing until one's application is approved in principle (either Quebec or Federal programs).

Processing delays under the federal program regularly exceed two and a half years. This reduces the incentive of the federal program. Rumor has it that the federal government wants to increase usage of its program and will reduce processing delays. Such rumors have come and gone in the past.

The Quebec program generally offers processing times in the area of 18 months or less to visa issuance, and 12 months to begin the five-year investment period from application submission.

As a result of the above factors, the majority of applicants use the Quebec program.

Applicants who require early entry may consider alternative methods of entering Canada on a non-immigrant work visa basis while waiting for permanent resident processing.

Canadian citizenship – a stepping stone to the USA

Canadian permanent residence does not confer any particular US immigration benefits. Canadian citizens may travel to the USA without a visa, and may seek employment in one year increments under the North American Free Trade Agreement (NAFTA). NAFTA provides a list of eligible classes of employment, most of which are executive, managerial, professional or scientific in nature. The USA does not offer Canadians a fast track to permanent residence, or employment outside of the NAFTA list.

Generally, one may apply for Canadian citizenship if one has lived in Canada three of the four years preceding the application. Canada, like most countries, excludes criminals from citizenship. Note that the Canadian definition of criminal includes people who have been convicted of driving while under the influence of alcohol.

Conclusion

Under the Canadian immigrant investor program, management experienced applicants may move to Canada for as little as $120,000 CDN. The down payment effectively becomes the cost of acquiring Canadian permanent residence. The relatively low entry costs make the Canadian program accessible to large numbers of people worldwide.

The largest advantage of the Canadian program is certainty. You know what it costs and, in most cases, you can be fairly certain whether or not you qualify. Processing times, now up to two years, need improvement. Depending upon your political point of view, the fact that the investment capital goes to provincial governments for public purposes is a good or bad thing. In any event, it's a certain thing.

Many people come to Canada as a stepping-stone to entry into the USA. The reality is not so clear. Canadians may not live in the USA for more than six months without a visa, and may not work in the USA without a visa permitting employment. While many Canadians maintain second homes in the USA, these homes may not be a primary residence. This is essentially no different from the US rules pertaining to the rest of the world. The rules for Canadians to obtain US permanent residence or citizenship are no different from the rules for anyone from any other country. The biggest advantage to using Canada as a stepping-stone is proximity. It's much easier to drive across the border to investigate a business, employment or investment opportunity than it is to fly across an ocean.

Acknowledgements

I would like to acknowledge the help of two of the most knowledgeable people in the business with this chapter. Colin Singer, an attorney based in Montreal, provided the legal point of view, while Eric Major, Assistant VP of HSBC Capital Canada Inc., provided insights to the financial aspects of the Canadian program. Please feel free to contact either of them if you have questions or need assistance.

HSBC Capital (Canada) Inc. ('HCCA') has been actively promoting the Canadian immigrant investor program since 1991 and has assisted over 2,500 investors and their families in immigrating to Canada. It has developed an expertise in the specialised area of immigration to Canada via the Investor category. It has established an extensive network of business introducers in key locations around the world, and leverages-off the bank's impressive global office network to source potential immigrant investors (HCCA is a member of HSBC Group). HSBC Group is one of the world's largest banking and financial services organizations, with over 9,500 offices in 79 countries and territories. It also has a comprehensive website (www.hsbc.ca/iip) that sources 20% of its investor clientele.

Colin R. Singer, Attorney, completed a law degree from the University of Ottawa in 1986 and was admitted to the Law Society of the Province of Quebec in 1988. He obtained a Bachelor's degree in 1982 from McGill University, majoring in industrial relations. In addition to being a founding director of the Canadian Citizenship & Immigration Resource Center (CCIRC) Inc., he is an Associate Editor of Immigration Law Reporter, the pre-eminent immigration law publication in Canada. He has previously served as an executive member of the Canadian Bar Association's Quebec and National Immigration Law Sections, and is currently a member of the Canadian Chapter of the American Immigration Lawyers Association. He has twice appeared before Canada's House of Commons Standing Committee on Citizenship and Immigration and is a frequent speaker at government and non-government immigration conferences.

Since 1994, he has provided ongoing guidance and opinions to readers on the Internet through www.immigration.ca, currently rated the most popular non-government Canadian immigration site by Alexa Internet, a subsidiary of Amazon.com.

5 · Carribean Sea Destinations

The Carribean Basin offers several island destinations. With the exception of Cuba, Puerto Rico and Hispanola (Haiti and the Dominican Republic), most of the islands are small, dry and sunny. The economy depends primarily on tourism, offshore banking in some cases, and a bit of mining and agriculture. Island life is laid back in the tropical style. The island populations consist of a mix of Europeans and descendents of black slaves. In virtually all cases, the original inhabitants have vanished.

History

The Caribbean Sea was first known to Europeans through Columbus who, thinking he was in India, landed at San Salvador in the Bahamas. It turns out that Columbus was a terrible navigator. Not only was he totally off on longitude, he was also well north of where he thought he was.

Over time, the Caribbean Basin islands were settled by Dutch, French, English, Spanish and Americans. While a few of the Caribbean Basin islands, such as US and British Virgin Islands, remain dependencies of other powers, most of the islands are now independent.

Overview

Virtually all of the Caribbean Basin Islands offer permanent residence through investment. The basic idea is to trade capital for economic development for second passports and/or a tropical island lifestyle. All of the popular destinations offer reasonable health care, air links to

Europe, South America and the US, and European or US standard housing. Generally, island living isn't cheap because virtually everything is imported and taxed. You may save on income taxes but you probably won't save on living expenses.

What follows is a summary of the immigrant investment programs of the more sought destinations. Destinations such as Barbados and the British Virgin Islands are not discussed because the rules are not clearly stated. Barbados will approve investments in real estate or small businesses for permanent residence but won't stipulate the conditions in advance. The British Virgin Islands use British law. The local authorities will grant permanent residence to investors whose programs they like; again, no clear guidance. Grenada, the island Ronald Reagan invaded to restore US pride, used to have an immigrant investment program and had a lucrative business in selling passports to Chinese. Due to external pressures, Grenada closed its passport and immigrant investment programs.

Federation of St Kitts and Nevis

St. Kitts and Nevis, two very small former British colonies, gained independence in 1983. The government is a constitutional democracy based on the British system, the national language is English, and the population is about 40,000. Most people choose St Kitts and Nevis for tax reasons and to procure a second passport.

St. Kitts and Nevis offer economic citizenship, which means you get a passport, but cannot work. To qualify, one can invest:

● US$200,000 in a ten year bond

● US$250,000 in an approved investment project

● US$150,000 in an approved investment project

Sometimes they run 'sales' when the investment amount goes to $50,000.

The offerings change so frequently that interested parties should contact authorities to get the current details.

Anguilla

Anguilla is a British dependency located near St. Kitts and Nevis. It's even smaller than St. Kitts and Nevis, with a population of about 12,000. There are two large problems with the Anguilla program. Investors must invest US$2,500,000 minimum and it takes ten years of residence to obtain citizenship.

Antigua and Barbuda

Antigua and Barbuda, also former British colonies, have a combined population of about 66,000, and both gained independence in 1981. On the islands, you simply buy a house to qualify. The basic steps are:

● Purchase or rent a residence.

● Pay stamp duties of 2.5% and foreign license fee of 5% of property value.

● Pay annual tax of US$20,000.

● Reside at least 30 days a year.

● Reside 30 days a year for seven years to become a citizen.

The Bahamas

The Bahamas, a hundred miles or so off the Florida coast, is a major tourist destination in its own right. The hundreds of islands offer world class resorts, fishing, beaches and gambling. There is also an established international investment and banking community. The Bahamas gained independence from Britain in 1973, is a member of the Commonwealth and has maintained a stable democratic government based on the British system.

The general requirements are:

● US$2 million net worth

● US$500,000 invested in the Bahamas for a period of 10 years, or

● Invest US$250,000 in a government-approved pooled program for five years.

One must reside in the Bahamas for at least 30 days per year.

Dominica

Dominica is a small island in the East Caribbean Sea. It's a former British dependency, now independent with a British style of government. Dominica is a beautiful island with lots of geographic diversity and a popular tourist destination, particularly for eco-tours. Dominica has modern communications and transportation infrastructure.

Dominica offers a second passport program. This is a passport like any other Dominican would have. Countries such as the USA have been known to deny entry to persons carrying Dominican passports who have no significant ties to Dominica. I know of several cases where Chinese and Russians using Dominican passports were denied entry to the USA.

The rules are simple. You buy it. One must make a gift to Dominica of US$50,000 which covers spouse and children under 18. Older children cost an additional US$10,000 each.

The other option is to buy a redeemable government bond with a principal value of US$75,000 paying 2% per annum in interest. In addition one must pay US$15,000 for the head of the household, US$10,000 for the spouse, US$10,000 for each child under 18, and US$15,000 for unmarried children between 18 and 25. Finally, the visa professionals got written into the law for a fee of US$14,500 payable only upon receipt of the passport. The good news is that there's no tax on offshore income. If you want a second passport, this is one of the easiest ways to obtain one.

Turks and Caicos

These 30 or so islands located to the south east of the Bahamas were part of the colony of Jamaica but separated after Jamaican independence. Turks and Caicos remains part of the United Kingdom and is administered as a foreign territory with internal autonomy. The basic industries are tourism, fishing and offshore financial services. To take advantage of the internal autonomy, the locals have created an immigrant investor program. The attraction is tropical living with no taxes.

Permanent residence, for those who don't want to work, may be obtained by buying a residence of at least US$250,000 in value in Providenciales, the main island, or US$125,000 elsewhere. Those who wish to invest in active trades or businesses can obtain the right to work. The investment amounts for approved businesses are US$250,000 in Providenciales and US$125,000 elsewhere.

Finally

I apologize in advance for either purposefully or unintentionally omitting somebody's favorite Caribbean destination. There are lots of opportunities for tropical living, in civilized locales, with convenient access to North America and Europe and without taxes. That's something to consider.

6 · Costa Rica

Retirees move to Costa Rica because of its nice weather, beaches and land-scape, high quality of life, good medical care and affordability. Costa Rica, traditionally the most stable government in Central America, is a constitutional democracy based on the US model. The country managed to avoid the civil wars in Guatamala, Nicaragua, Panama and Salvador, to name a few. Spanish is the national language but English is generally spoken. There is a large North American ex-pat community that provides an accessible social network.

Costa Rica is a popular eco-tour destination for North Americans. Eco-tours include jungle flora and fauna, tropical beaches and bird-watching. Anglers from all over the world come to Costa Rica for a variety of game fishing on the Pacific and Caribbean coasts. The climate ranges from tropical on the coasts to temperate in the central highlands. San Jose, the capital, lies in the central plateau and enjoys spring-like weather most of the year. Several mountain ranges run from north to south, with the highest peaks reaching 3800 meters.

Obtaining immigrant status

To obtain immigrant status, one can either invest or prove a stream of income from a pension or private investments sufficient to support one-self without working in Costa Rica. Permanent residents can manage their own investments and work in companies in which they invested. They may use local health care, which is of high quality and reasonably priced compared to the USA, and is in large part US-trained. Permanent residents under the Resident Annuitants and Resident Pensioners categories pay no income tax in Costa Rica but pay local and property taxes. Retirees may not seek employment or other remuner-ated activities in the country. Costa Rica recognizes dual citizenship, which is available after seven years of permanent residency. For people from Spain and Central America, the requirement is five years.

There are two basic programs applicable to immigrant investors or passive investors. 'Resident Annuitants' and 'Resident Pensioners' categories permit people with guaranteed income to become permanent residents. Alternatively, immigrants may invest at least US$50,000 in a variety of projects described below.

The resident annuitants and resident pensioners law

This law – in two parts, *Pensionado* and *Rentista* – applies to individuals who can prove a permanent and stable income from investments, pension or retirement plans.

On an ongoing basis, *Pensionado* and *Rentista* immigrants must:

● Prove on an annual basis that the required funds were exchanged into local currency

● Reside a minimum of four months in the country per year.

Pensionado

The *Pensionado* applicant must demonstrate a permanent income stream from a pension or similiar source of at least US$600 per month. Typically, applicants rely upon national pension, or corporate pension benefits.

Rentista

The *Rentista* applicant must prove a permanent fixed income of at least US$1,000 per month for a period of five years, from investment income rather than a pension. Applicants must certify the existence of their income stream by bank reference letters, proof of property ownership, or accountant reports. The authorities require a higher income stream due to the perceived less secure nature of the source of income. The investment funds may be held abroad. The sponsoring bank or investment institution must state that the applicant will receive US$1,000 per month in Costa Rica, in a manner that is stable and irrevocable, for at least five years, and that the financial institution will notify the Costa Rican immigration department (*Dirección General de Migración y Extranjería*) if the funds are withdrawn or financial conditions change.

The investor program

Individuals who invest at least US$50,000 in a project which is approved by the Center for the Promotion of Exports (PROCOMER) as a priority investment area, may qualify for **resident investor status**. Priority investments include tourism, reforestation or other projects in the national interest.

This category involves two different steps. The first is to ask PRO-COMER to determine if the investment falls within the priority area. Once this initial process has been completed and the certification issued, you then begin the permanent residency application process, which is done directly before the Department of Immigration.

If the investment is in a non-priority investment area, then the required investment is US$200,000. Even so, the investment must be made in an approved list of business categories, which include ornamental flowers, leather, spices, processed foods, wood products, mining or production of capital goods. The list changes from time to time; this description is merely illustrative, not exhaustive. Investors must spend at least six months per year in Costa Rica.

Conclusion

Costa Rica offers rule of law, secure immigration status, temperate climate and excellent medical care at very reasonable prices. Many North Americans come to know the country through eco-tours and end up making Costa Rica their retirement home. Pension checks simply go further in Costa Rica. For those who need a dose of North America, there are several daily flights to Miami of about two hours, and most other major North American cities.

Acknowledgements

Many thanks to Arcelio Hernandez, who took the time to edit this article.

Arcelio Hernandez, Attorney at Law, Costa Rica. Email: info@forovial.com. Website: www.forovial.com. Telephone: 506 365 3088.

7 · Fiji

Fiji offers immigrant investors access to an English-speaking South Pacific paradise. The ex-pat community includes Koreans, Japanese, Chinese, as well as Europeans and North Americans. Fiji offers world-class golf, beaches and fishing. Social, banking and communications services, although not up to European standard, do the job. The down side is political instability and occasional ethnic violence between Fijians and Indians. To date, foreigners seem to be exempt from the fray. As long as immigration remains a trickle rather than a socially upsetting flood, the atmosphere should remain conducive to investors looking for quality of life.

There are two non-immigrant visas appropriate for investors: resident permits and investor permits.

Residence permit

Residence permit applicants must invest in any business venture of over F$100,000 approved by the Fiji Islands Trade and Investment Bureau. They must also prove disposable assets outside Fiji sufficient to ensure that they will not become a public charge or need to seek employment in the Fiji Islands.

A summary of the rules follows:

● The principal applicant must be at least 45 years of age and carry health insurance.

● The principal applicant should have an assured income and should not seek employment in the Fiji Islands.

- The principal applicant must deposit a sum of F$140,000 in a resident account of a local bank upon approval of the application, as well as purchase a bond of F$2,063 for each family member.

- Real estate is no longer included in the investment amount.

- The permit holder must obtain clearance from the Immigration Department for any repatriation of funds used to qualify for immigration status and be willing to give up immigration status as a result.

- The applicant must have adequate knowledge of the English language.

In summary, one merely makes a bank deposit of F$140,000 and receives a three-year residence permit in return. To renew for another three years, simply show that you have F$30,000 in cash in Fiji for a family of up to three dependents under age 45, or F$40,000 for families of four or more dependents under age 45.

One may not remove the investment funds from Fiji without government permission unless one is also giving up the residence permit. Citizenship laws change often; currently one must live in Fiji five out of ten years. Because Fiji doesn't permit dual nationality, few people bother to apply.

Investor permit

The investor permit is same as the residence permit but requires a F$250,000 investment in return for a seven-year stay, rather than three years as in the case of the residence permit. Investors may apply for citizenship after five years' continuous residence.

Permanent residency permit

The Fijian government introduced the permanent residency permit to help foreign entrepreneurs come and go as they please, and obtain assurance that they can stay in Fiji without applying for citizenship and losing their overseas nationality.

The rules are as follows.

1. The applicant:

   ● Must be of good fame and character

   ● Cannot vote or take part in politics

   ● Can have unrestricted length of residence as long as the conditions of the permit are not breached.

2. If the applicant applies for a permit to reside on assured income, he/she:

   ● Must have purchased a property costing no less than F$75,000 in Fiji

   ● Must have proof of a regular assured income derived from an overseas source of at least $F25,000 per annum

   ● Cannot take up employment without securing a work permit.

3. If the applicant applies for an investor permit, he/she:

   ● Must have introduced investment capital of not less than F$250,000

   ● May be employed in the investment project, but for employment elsewhere it will be necessary to obtain a work permit.

4. Spouses and children of the applicant who are 21 years and under qualify for the same permanent residence permit.

Most readers will have no problem with the financial requirements, have little desire to participate in Fijian politics, and do not wish to seek Fijian employment. The only obstacle to obtaining this visa is convincing somebody who has never heard of you that you are of 'good fame and character'. This problem is best solved by applying through a connected migration agent.

Conclusion

Fiji offers one of the best combinations of infrastructure, golf, fishing and lifestyle in the tropical South Pacific. Those with sufficient funds and no criminal record should have little problem obtaining immigration status. Housing is reasonably priced, of relatively high quality and readily available.

As strange as its seems, the more effective migration agents for Fijian purposes are based in Seoul, Korea.

Acknowledgements

Young Kang of Nammi Emmigration provided the material for this chapter. Email: ykang@2min.com. Telephone: 822 725 5993.

8 · France

Due to France's many attractions, such as being one of the world's culinary centers, and the romantic notion of Paris and the French Riviera, many US citizens and other foreign nationals wish to retire or take an extended holiday in the country. The last thing on their minds is the immigration rules and regulations that govern their stay. To encourage investment and business development, the French immigration service does accommodate those foreigners who wish to take up residence in France but have no intentions to work during their stay. The French immigration service is a flexible, ever-changing system that lacks clear immigration procedures. Sometimes immigration matters are taken on a case-by-case basis.

This chapter will focus on the French visa category that allows an individual to remain in France for an extended stay without filing a work permit application.

Immigration policy

French Immigration requires that all persons (other than French citizens, French permanent residents and European Union citizens) who will be taking up gainful employment obtain employment authorization prior to entering France, with limited exceptions. EU nationals are not required to obtain work permits and are no longer required to obtain a resident permit called a *Carte de Sejour*. They may freely work and reside in France (an EU policy that aims to promote the free movement of people and trade within EU borders).

Non-EU citizens

Citizens of the US and visa exempt nationals are not required to obtain visas prior to entering France, but must indicate to the immigration officer in the Primary Inspection Line at the port of entry that they are coming to France as a business visitor. Business visitors cannot have intent to join the French labor market. Their principal place of business and their primary remuneration source must be outside of France. Permissible business activities for a typical business visitor are business meetings, negotiations, business or professional conventions, consulting, research and soliciting of business.

Citizens who require a visa must obtain a Schengen visa or business visa prior to their arrival in France, from the French consulate having jurisdiction over their place of residence. Business visitors and tourists will be admitted into France either for the duration of their temporary visit (as indicated in a corporate support letter), or for a maximum period of 90 days within a six-month period starting from the date of their first entry into France. However, if an employee is admitted to France under a visitor status, he or she may not be lawfully employable without first obtaining a work permit. This employee will not be able to change to employment status while in France. Importantly, there are no extensions of the 90-day period unless there is an urgent reason, such as health or family emergency.

It is important to note that the 90-day time period is inclusive of all the Schengen territories which include: Austria, Belgium, Denmark, Finland, France, Germany, Greece, Iceland, Italy, Luxembourg, the Netherlands, Norway, Portugal, Spain and Sweden. Under the Schengen Agreement, time is cumulative. Thus, if an individual went to France for two months starting February 1, 2004, then traveled to the United Kingdom, which is not part of the Schengen territories, for one month, he or she could return to France for one more month during the six-month period, or until July 31, 2004. However, if after spending two months in France the individual spent the month of April in Germany, he or she would have capped-out the 90-day period and would not be able to return to France.

General visa qualifications and application procedures

There is only one French visa category that allows for an individual to reside in France and not obtain the appropriate work visa, as France does not have an investor visa. If you wish to invest in France, you will need to file a long-stay visitor visa application at the French consulate having jurisdiction over your place of residence. There is no minimum amount of investment required with this type of application. However, the French government must be assured that the investor will be creating jobs for French citizens or otherwise demonstrate a positive impact on the French economy.

You must file an application form along with evidence that you meet the eligibility requirements or proof of financial support. You must provide a support letter that substantiates your means and ability to invest as well as financial statements to support this statement. You must also obtain the appropriate letter of invitation from France. In addition, you need to provide evidence of citizenship such as a valid passport. If you are in the US in a non-immigrant visa category, you must provide evidence of valid US immigration status such as an H-1B visa endorsed in the passport, an I-94 card, and an H-1B petition approval, I-797. You will need to provide two passport sized photographs and a government filing fee to process the application. The consulate generally will want to see proof of residency while in France, such as a copy of a rental agreement or proof of purchase of a home, i.e. a title or deed. Importantly, the consulate will want to see proof of medical insurance while overseas. Upon receipt of the visa application at the French consulate, the processing time ranges from one week to several months.

Once you arrive in France with your long-stay visitor visa status, you must apply at the local police precinct or *prefecture* within eight days of arrival for a resident permit called a *Carte de Sejour*. The *Carte de Sejour* will allow you to freely travel in and out of France and to reside in France. Medical exams will be required as part of the *Carte de Sejour* application process. The first *Carte de Sejour* is issued for one year and is renewable annually under the visitor immigration status. The processing time is approximately six to eight weeks but may be longer depending on how busy the particular *prefecture* is at the time of submission. If you have long-stay visitor immigration status, you have few rights and this visa category does not lead to permanent residence. If you are applying as managing director of a company, it is recommended that you change status to a *commercant* or *salarié*, which will allow you to seek permanent residence status after five consecutive years under such immigration status.

Dependents filed at the French consulate

Generally, the spouse and unmarried dependent children are included on the principal employee's visa application at the French consulate. A personal appearance may be required by the French consulate for each family member and is discretionary. Spouses must find their own independent employer if they wish to work while residing in France. *Cartes de Sejour* are not issued to dependent children under the age of 16.

Conclusion

As the French immigration system is not always straightforward, additional documentation may be requested throughout the process. It is imperative that you provide complete and thorough visa applications. If you do not provide sufficient supporting documentation, your application may be denied, potentially resulting in significant hardship to yourself and accompanying family members. An individual entering France for a short business trip or for employment must be in lawful immigration status. You should never enter as a tourist when you are representing a company.

Although historically there has been little enforcement of French immigration regulations, the climate is changing throughout the world, and we can expect to see further changes in France. You are advised to comply strictly with the law in order to avoid damaging consequences to both yourself and your accompanying family members.

Acknowledgements

Deborah B. Davy manages the Global Visa Group specializing in global visas and global compliance at Berry, Appleman & Leiden. She is skilled at managing high-volume international personnel transfers, both for short-term and long-term assignments, for large multinational companies in the high technology, manufacturing and financial sectors. She specializes in assisting global corporations in designing, developing and implementing successful international visa programs. Ms Davy has established strong working relationships with the premier service providers worldwide and has an encyclopedic knowledge of the rules and procedures associated with global visa and work permit processes. Ms Davy received her J.D. from Thomas Jefferson School of Law and was admitted to the California Bar in 1997. She was Law Review Editor-in-Chief of the San Diego Justice Journal. She competed in the Phillip C. Jessup International Moot Court Competition. She is a member of American Immigration Lawyers Association and is a frequent speaker on global visa practice issues.

9 · Italy

The attractions of Italy's Tuscany, with its rolling vineyards, haystacks and sunflowers, not to mention its wonderful food, mean that many United States citizens and other foreign nationals wish to retire or take an extended holiday in Italy. Similar to the USA, Italy is subject to a quota system to restrict the number of foreign workers. To encourage investment and business development, the Italian immigration service does accommodate those foreigners who wish to take up residence in Italy but have no intention to work during their stay. The Italian immigration service is a flexible, ever-changing system that lacks clear immigration procedures. Sometimes immigration matters are taken on a case-by-case basis.

This chapter will focus on the Italian visa categories that allow an individual to remain in Italy for an extended stay without filing a work permit application – Elective Residence and Autonomous visas.

Immigration policy

Italian Immigration requires that all persons (other than Italian citizens, Italian permanent residents and European Union citizens) who will be taking up gainful employment obtain employment authorization prior to entering Italy, with limited exceptions. EU nationals are not required to obtain work permits, but apply for a *carte di soggorno* within 90 days. They may freely live and reside in Italy (an EU policy that aims to promote the free movement of people and trade within EU borders).

Non-EU citizens

Citizens of the US and visa exempt nationals are not required to obtain visas prior to entering Italy, but must indicate to the immigration officer in the Primary Inspection Line at the port of entry that they are coming to Italy as a business visitor. Business visitors cannot have intent to join the Italian labor market. Their principal place of business and their primary remuneration source must be outside of Italy. Permissible business activities for a typical business visitor are business meetings, negotiations, business or professional conventions, consulting, research and soliciting of business.

Citizens who require a visa must obtain a Schengen visa or business visa prior to their arrival in Italy, from the Italian consulate having jurisdiction over their place of residence. Business visitors and tourists will be admitted into Italy either for the duration of their temporary visit (as indicated in a corporate support letter) or for a maximum period of 90 days within a six-month period starting from the date of their first entry into Italy. However, if an employee is admitted to Italy under a visitor status, he or she may not be lawfully employable without first obtaining a work permit. This employee will not be able to change to employment status while in Italy. Importantly, there are no extensions of the 90-day period unless there is an urgent reason, such as health or family emergency.

It is important to note that the 90-day time period is inclusive of all the Schengen territories which include: Austria, Belgium, Denmark, Finland, France, Germany, Greece, Iceland, Italy, Luxembourg, the Netherlands, Norway, Portugal, Spain, and Sweden. Under the Schengen Agreement time is cumulative. Thus, if an individual went to Italy for two months starting February 1, 2004, then traveled to the United Kingdom, which is not part of the Schengen territories, for one month, he or she could return to Italy for one more month during the six-month period, or until July 31, 2004. However, if after spending two months in Italy the individual spent the month of April in Germany, he or she would have capped-out the 90-day period and would not be able to return to Italy

General visa qualifications and application procedures

There are a limited number of Italian visa categories that allow an individual to reside in Italy without obtaining a work visa. The two main visa categories are the Elective Residence Visa and the Autonomous Worker Visa.

Elective Residence Visa

Both applications require the visa application be filed at the Italian consulate having jurisdiction over your place of residence. The first visa category, Elective Residence Visa or *Residenza Elettiva,* allows the individual to enter Italy for an open-term visit. This visa is for those foreigners who intend to take up residence in Italy and plan to support themselves autonomously without obtaining an employer-supported work permit. You must file an application form along with evidence that you meet the eligibility requirements or proof of financial support. You must demonstrate this through original financial documents such as bank statements, investment or brokerage statements from associated firms, and social security statements, which state current balances in the accounts.

These balances cannot be derived from your current employer or from activity that will be performed by you in Italy. You must be able to demonstrate that the payment for your home while in Italy will not be earned while you are in Italy. The source of income must come from an investment portfolio. The consulate will review the account balances to confirm that they are sufficient and 'more than substantial' to support you for the duration of stay or the equivalent of approximately US$2,500 to US$3,000 per month.

You must also provide evidence of citizenship such as a valid passport. If you are in the US in a non-immigrant visa category, you must provide evidence of valid US immigration status such as an H-1B visa endorsed in the passport, a I-94 card, and an H-1B petition approval, I-797. You will need to provide two passport sized photographs and a government filing fee to process the application. The consulate generally will want to see proof of housing availability while in Italy such as a copy of a rental agreement or proof of purchase of a home, i.e. a title or deed. You will also need to provide a Certificate of Good Conduct or police certificate indicating you do not have a police record. This is generally obtained from a police precinct having jurisdiction over your home residence. The consulate will want to see proof of medical insurance while overseas. Upon receipt of the visa application at the Italian consulate, the processing time ranges from one week to several months.

Autonomous Visa

If you want to be self-employed in Italy there is an Autonomous Visa category called *Lavoro Autonomo*. This category is subject to a quota of 2,500 autonomous workers for 2004, in accordance with Article 27 of the Italian Immigration Law. In order to enter Italy as an independent worker, you must obtain a license or statement that certifies that you meet the qualifications and requirements for your profession. This license or statement can be obtained from either 1) the Chamber of Commerce for commercial activities; 2) the professional roster for liberal professions; or 3) filed directly with the local police precinct or *questura*. If it is filed directly with the *questura*, you must provide an employment contract along with the certificate of registration of the sending company, which must be legalized at the Italian consulate. You must provide a declaration by the company to the Labor Office, which expressly states that 'there will be no dependent work relationship' between you and the company. The *Direzione Provinciale del Lavoro* must endorse this declaration. In addition, you must demonstrate that your income exceeds the minimum wage granted by the Italian government. You also need to provide a copy of the company's most recent budget and federal tax returns.

Generally, the Italian consulate requires you to come in person to file this application. You must complete an application form and submit an original passport and notarized copy of a driver's license or state ID as proof of residence in the consulate's jurisdiction. You must provide a copy of the application submitted to the *questura* and the approved *Nulla Osta*. The consulate requires proof of a home rental agreement, or proof of purchase of a home through a title or deed, as well as evidence of stated income, which must exceed the minimum wage that the Italian government provides for public assistance. Lastly, the consulate requires a copy of the travel itinerary evidencing that travel is imminent. The consulate will also request a government-filing fee.

If you are a corporate executive or partner of an Italian based company, you must provide the Italian consulate with sufficient documentation demonstrating your senior position in the company – organization charts, Board of Resolution, job description, resumé showing experience and education and other corporate documentation. This documentation is in addition to the documentation discussed above under the Autonomous Visa.

Importantly, all foreigners who wish to reside in Italy and enter in either the Elective Residence Visa or the Autonomous Worker Visa category must register their arrival within eight days of entry at the police precinct or *questura* having jurisdiction over their Italian residence.

Dependents filed at the Italian consulate

Generally, your spouse and unmarried dependent children are included on your visa application at the Italian consulate. A personal appearance may be required by the Italian consulate for each family member and is discretionary. Spouses must find their own independent employer if they wish to work while residing in Italy.

Conclusion

As Italian immigration is never straightforward, additional documentation may be requested throughout the process. It is imperative that you provide complete and thorough visa applications. If you do not provide sufficient supporting documentation, your application may be denied, potentially resulting in significant hardship to yourself and accompanying family members. An individual entering Italy for a short business trip or for employment must be in a lawful immigration status. You should never enter as a tourist when you are representing a company.

Although historically there has been little enforcement of Italian immigration regulations, the climate is changing throughout the world, and we can expect to see further changes in Italy. You are advised to comply strictly with the law in order to avoid damaging consequences to both yourself and accompanying family members.

Acknowledgements

Deborah B. Davy manages the Global Visa Group specializing in global visas and global compliance at Berry, Appleman & Leiden. She is skilled at managing high-volume international personnel transfers, both for short-term and long-term assignments, for large multinational companies in the high technology, manufacturing and financial sectors. She specializes in assisting global corporations in designing, developing and implementing successful international visa programs. Ms Davy has established strong working relationships with the premier service providers worldwide and has an encyclopedic knowledge of the rules and proce-dures associated with global visa and work permit processes. Ms Davy received her J.D. from Thomas Jefferson School of Law and was admitted to the California Bar in 1997. She was Law Review Editor-in-Chief of the San Diego Justice Journal. She competed in the Phillip C. Jessup International Moot Court Competition. She is a member of American Immigration Lawyers Association and is a frequent speaker on global visa practice issues.

10 · Malaysia

Malaysia offers beautiful tropical beaches as well as temperate mountain climates. The population is well educated and English is widely spoken. Malaysia is a Muslim country with Islam as the official religion. The country has an advanced infrastructure, high tech industrial base and an excellent educational system. The political system is stable in the sense that the same group has run the country since anybody can remember, but unstable in the sense that there is no organized and peaceable method of venting opposing views or changing the succession of power. The government tends to favor the ethnic Malays, who they feel have been historically exploited by European colonists, Chinese and Indians.

English language education

Very few quality of life immigrants choose Malaysia for political, ethnic or religious reasons. Most Asians seek Malaysian status to obtain reasonably priced English language education for their children. Applicants may not work in Malaysia without special permission and students must obtain a 'student pass' to attend school. Student passes are easily obtained because Malaysia promotes its educational system to foreign students. Retirees avail themselves of the investment scheme to take advantage of beautiful beaches and pleasant hill country.

Requirements of Malaysia's investment scheme

● Married applicants over 50 years of age must deposit RM 150,000 in a local bank **or** prove monthly income from outside sources of RM 10,000 or more

- Unmarried applicants over 50 years of age must deposit RM 100,000 in a local bank **or** prove monthly income from outside sources of RM 7,000 or more

- Married applicants under 50 years of age must deposit RM 150,000 in a local bank **and** prove monthly income from outside sources of RM 10,000 or more

- Unmarried applicants under 50 years of age must deposit RM 100,000 in a local bank **and** prove monthly income from outside sources of RM 7,000 or more

Applicants receive a five-year multiple entry visa and must maintain their deposit to renew. Visas must be sponsored by a licensed local organization. The scheme includes children under 18 who are not going to school in Malaysia and one maid. As stated above, students need a student pass. Essentially, applicants buy a five-year stay in Malayasia by making the above listed financial commitments.

Conclusion

To summarize, Malaysia's immigrant investor program is focused toward those who wish to obtain a reasonably priced and high quality English language education for their children. Most people looking for a quality of life venue without the political overtones in South East Asia choose Thailand.

Acknowledgements

Special thanks again to Young Kang, of Nammi Immigration, Seoul Korea, who edited this chapter and has particular expertise in obtaining Malaysian immigration status on behalf of retirees. Telephone: 822 725 5993. Email: ykang@2min.com

11 · Malta

Malta, located in the center of the Mediterranean Sea, to the east of Sicily, has played a key role in European history since Crusader times. The island has been ruled by Muslims, the Holy Roman Empire, Knights of St John and the British to name a few. The climate is dry and warm, with rainy cool winters. Maltese cuisine reflects its varied past. English is the language of commerce and education. Housing, even beach front and view housing, is very reasonable. One can find nice, well-located flats for US$100,000. The capital city, Valletta, offers all of the conveniences of any European capital. Now that Malta is part of the European Union, its citizens can access virtually all of Europe.

Permanent residence

Malta offers among the more flexible permanent residence packages, along with European Union membership as of 2004. Malta offers the convenience of English language, good schools, nice weather and visa-free access to Europe. As a result of EU membership and favorable taxation, many non-EU citizens use Malta as a gateway to Europe. For example, many Asians obtain Maltese permanent residency to access UK education for their children and to access UK markets for their goods. The fact that English is widely spoken also attracts people for educational purposes. The main requirement is to invest at least MTL 30,000 (US$70,000) in a flat.

Malta's lenient permanent residence program hopes to attract financially sophisticated foreigners to settle on the island. The stated hope is that the new immigrants would bring foreign exchange and generate income for the economy. Malta's investment immigrant program dates from 1960, with the current program in place since 1988.

The rules

Permanent residence status requires:

● An annual income equivalent to 10,000 Maltese lira (1 MTL = approx. US$ 2.50), or ownership of capital equivalent to MTL 150,000; *and*

● Annual remittance to Malta from abroad of a minimum MTL 6,000, plus MTL 1,000 for each dependent.

'Dependents' means spouse, children under 21 years of age and a parent or grandparent who is wholly dependent on the applicant.

Once in possession of the permit, the resident must, within the first year after obtaining the permit:

1. Enter Malta to have the passport stamped and register with the Inland Revenue Department.–

2. Either purchase a flat valued at least MTL 30,000; *or*

   – Purchase a house valued at least MTL 50,000; *or*

   – Rent property for at least MTL 1,800 per annum.

Additionally, permanent residents may not engage in business, freelance work or employment nor engage in any form of political activity in Malta. Permanent residents may use Malta as a base to work from provided that they market their goods or services abroad. Malta does not require permanent residents to reside in Malta for a minimum period of time. Consequently, Maltese permanent residence status does not automatically confer EU immigration and right to work benefits.

Upon the death of the permanent resident, the residence permit is transmitted to the surviving spouse, but does not pass on to the descendants upon the death of the spouse.

Tax advantages

● A flat rate of **15% tax** subject to a minimum tax liability of MTL 1,800 (approx. Euro 4,500) per family.

● No tax on worldwide income or assets.

- No inheritance taxes.

- No capital gains tax arising outside Malta.

- There is an exit tax on repatriated proceeds of sale of real estate of 35%.

Conclusion

Most people come to Malta for business reasons, i.e. to establish a company with access to Europe, in a low tax jurisdiction. The weather and generally superior quality of life also attracts those who want a second home with access to Europe. The authorities are generally helpful and welcoming to immigrants. The local population is also pro-immigrant and pro-commerce.

Acknowledgements

Special thanks to Young Kang of Nammi Emmigration, Seoul, Korea. Telephone: 822 725 5993. Email: ykang@2min.com

12 · Mexico

People generally retire to Mexico for warm weather, fishing, swimming, hiking and cheap living. A couple can live very well, with servants, for US$2,000 per month. In fact one can live quite well on half that amount. Medical care is of high quality and a fraction of the cost for the same services in the USA. Most Mexican professionals speak English. Long-term residents can apply for the state-run medical system which only costs US$200 per year. Mexico has a reasonable freeway system, mostly toll roads. One can drive through most of the country with relative ease. Note that most US insurance policies exclude driving in Mexico. You can purchase car insurance in Mexico or purchase special riders in the USA.

Geography

Mexico is a large country, half again larger than Texas, with Carribean and Pacific coastlines. The north of the country is a desert, and several mountain ranges run from north to south. Most of the population live in the mountains because the weather is drier and cooler as opposed to very hot and dry in the desert and very hot and humid in much of the coastal areas. The capital, Mexico City, with a population estimated to exceed 23 million, lies in the mountainous center of the country. The total population is estimated to be 103 million, the vast majority indigenous. Mexico City is quite cosmopolitan with fantastic art galleries, Aztec ruins and grand boulevards of the French style. Guadalajara, the industrial second city, lies in the mountainous north west part of the country. Oaxaca, an enchanting native town, lies directly to the south of Mexico City on essentially the same mountain range. Oaxaca is probably the best place to see Native American markets, ruins and historical artifacts. The Carribean coast features nice beaches with a hot and humid climate, while the Pacific coast is a bit drier but also hot.

The most popular areas of Mexico for retirees are Cancun and the coast to the south called the Costa Maya; the Pacific Coast including Puerto Vallerta, and lesser known Puerto Escondido, as well as fashionable Cabo San Lucas; and the central highlands, particularly San Miguel de Allende, a restored colonial town, and Lake Chapala near Guadalajara.

Cancun and Cozumel are well-known tourist destinations located on the Caribbean coast. The coastal highway heading south passes through several small beach towns with great snorkeling and fishing. Many foreigners own or rent homes along this coastal road. The road ends at a national park open to beachcombing and fishing.

Lake Chapala, located 30 miles south of Guadalajara, is Mexico's largest lake, roughly 55 miles long and 15 miles wide. This area benefits from cool evenings and comfortable daytime temperatures. Originally settled by the Spanish in the early 1500s, the area became a retirement haven shortly after the Second World War. Most people live in Ajijic, a well-kept colonial town of about 5,000 people. There's plenty of shopping, nightlife and restaurants. Guadalajara, a large industrial city, is about a half hour drive away.

San Miguel de Allende is a restored colonial town a few hours by car from Mexico City. The town may have more foreign than local residents. This is probably the most popular and expensive retirement destination in Mexico.

Puerto Vallerta and Cabo San Lucas, at the tip of Baja California, are Pacific coast beach towns. Both cities cater to retirees, offering plenty of shopping, nightlife and beach oriented activities. There are numerous small beach towns, such as Puerto Escondido, on the Pacific coast to the west of Oaxaca, frequented by retirees. Life in these towns is slower and more tranquil. The smaller the town, the greater the chance of sporadic electric power, difficult roads and air links, and sparse health care.

History

The Spanish invaded and began to settle in Mexico in the early 1500s. They encountered native American civilizations (Aztec, Maya and Tolmec) that had erected advanced cities, temples, roads and irrigation networks. On the other hand, most of the tribes practised human sacrifice and slavery and were quite warlike. These tribes were ruled by small groups of elites. The Spanish managed to conquer all of the Native American civilizations leaving the few pyramids, grave sites and ruins people visit today. The vast majority of the natives died of smallpox. Most of the survivors were enslaved to work in gold and silver mines and converted to Christianity. While some Europeans, mostly Spanish, settled in Mexico, and continue to dominate economic and social life, the vast majority of the Mexican population is descended from the native cultures conquered by the Spanish. There are parts of Mexico where most people speak Maya or other native languages and not Spanish.

As a rule, Mexicans are very polite, hard working and nice. While illiteracy runs high among the Native populations, enough English is spoken in the towns to suffice for daily needs. If you get into an intellectual discussion, you will find that many Mexicans blame the USA for their economic and social problems. The most familiar refrain is that the USA stole most of the country, which is true, and actively seeks to keep the country poor, not true. Mexico was a richer and more prosperous country than the USA until the 19th century. For whatever reason, most likely the lack of rule of law, there was no indigenous industrial revolution in Mexico.

The country included most of the American West from Texas up to Oregon. These territories were lost in stages, but the last deed was done in the 1840s when General Winfield Scott, with a very small army, managed to duplicate Cortez's feat and conquered Mexico City. Other than banditry, alien smuggling and drug dealing, the US-Mexican border has been relatively peaceful ever since.

While the US did relieve Mexico of more than half of its territory, the remaining lands are very fertile and blessed with copious natural resources, including oil, and a very nice climate. You might think that a country that is naturally rich can't blame economic woes entirely on outside forces.

Lifestyle

Despite the history, Mexico is an excellent retirement destination, and people are generally quite pleasant. This doesn't mean one can walk anywhere at night in Mexico City. Home owners should have security systems for burglars. There are a fair amount of pickpockets and purse thieves. These problems may be found anywhere, maybe a bit more in Mexico, but not at a level to deter a retiree.

Purchasing property

Mexican residential property in the coastal or border zones can be legally purchased by foreigners, but only through the *fideicomiso* (bank trust) method. Property in other areas of the country is, with few exceptions, not available to foreigners. The trusts last for 50 years, and are automatically renewable (for a nominal fee) at the end of the term. You have virtually all the rights of ownership, including passing the property by will or through the trust document to heirs. The major condition is that the property may only be used for residential purposes. Mexico has lots of laws and regulations and as many ways around them, including bribes. If you intend to purchase property in Mexico, be sure to do your homework.

Visa options

Those intending to spend more than six months in Mexico generally apply for a FM-3 visa or *Rentista*. The FM-T permits short-term visitors to come and go during a six-month period. Immigrants obtain an FM-2 visa.

To qualify for a *Rentista*, you must be over 50 years of age. The visa is issued initially for one year and can be renewed four more times for a period of one year. After the five-year period one may apply for permanent residence without further qualification. Permanent residents in Mexico have all the rights of citizens except the right to vote. Permanent residents do not need to surrender their passport, and may use their own passport to return home. If you stay outside of Mexico for longer than two years, or for five years in any 10-year period, you will lose your resident status in Mexico.

Requirements to apply for a permit to reside in Mexico on a permanent basis (non-immigrant *rentista*)

1. **Valid passport** with at least one full unused visa page and valid for at least one year.

2. **Photos**: two recent, front view, 2"×2", color with white background.

3. **Health certificate**: issued by the family doctor, stating that the applicant, as well as the dependents, do not have any contagious diseases (notarized).

4. **Letter from police department**: indicating that there is no police record (notarized).

5. **Notarized letter from a bank or financial institution** stating the source of your monthly income. Monthly income must be US$1,000 minimum, plus US$500 for each dependent. The monthly income requirement equals 400 times the daily minimum wage in Mexico. If the applicant is married and has dependents, certified copies of the marriage certificate and the birth certificates of all dependents are required. Children over 18 years of age are not considered dependents unless they are students or have a physical disability. If a dependent is not the wife or one of the children of the applicant, the applicant must prove that s/he has supported the dependent for a least one full year. The letter must also specify how the money is going to be available to the applicant while in Mexico.

6. **Fee**: immigration fee for the FM3 is US$74.

All documents submitted must be originals, the date of issue not more than 60 days ago and duly notarized. **All visas must be used within three months from the date issued.**

Conclusion

While most of the retirees come from the USA and Canada, many Europeans have discovered Mexico. One could easily immerse oneself in the ex-pat network and never experience Mexican culture. That would be a shame because

Mexico offers a rich cultural life. The country is large and varied, which creates many choices of retirement location. One can fly to any city in the world from Mexico City. Regional cities all have frequent flights to points in the USA and Canada. The local infrastructure for immigration matters, car insurance, medical insurance and purchasing a home is well established, and excepting some frustrating inefficiencies, does the job. Mexico offers a great quality of life at a very reasonable price.

13 · New Zealand

New Zealand reminds me very much of my home, Seattle, Washington, in the Pacific Northwest of the United States. The North Island offers a temperate climate with lush foliage. The South Island, a bit colder, offers spectacular mountain scenery. It's paradise for fishers and golfers. The New Zealand brown trout, originally bred at the University of Washington in Seattle, grows to giant size in New Zealand's lakes and rivers. Golf courses are plentiful, of high quality and are very cheap by European and even North American standards. The local wines are of very high quality, particularly the Pinot Noir varieties. The cuisine, generally European style, is also excellent. The locals are friendly and generally welcoming to immigrants.

The government is a parliamentary democracy similar to the system in the UK. Social services and education are of high quality and the bulk of the population would be considered middle class. There are few rich people in world terms and few poor people, or at least one doesn't see them. The government actively seeks to recruit immigrants mostly to fill skills needs. The investor program is designed to attract skilled business people as well as capital.

History

The Maoris, who inhabited New Zealand before the arrival of the Europeans, sailed south from what is now Hawaii around 800 AD. A further migration occurred around 1350. The Maoris, a warrior race, quickly subdued the local inhabitants and occupied what is now New Zealand, many small surrounding islands and the Chatham Islands. They practised cannibalism in that they made ritual feasts of their victims. The population of the Chatham Islands was decimated in this way.

The arrival of Europeans

The first European to note the existence of New Zealand was the Dutch explorer Abel Tasman in 1642. The Dutch evidently knew of the existence of the New Zealand islands from Portuguese and Venetian maps. Tasman abandoned his attempts to settle the islands when many of his landing party were eaten. Since that time whalers stopped in New Zealand, many never to be heard from again. In 1769, Captain James Cook circumnavigated the North and South Islands on his way to Australia. Cook recommended New Zealand for European habitation and believed the Maoris could be turned into industrious European-type settlers. Cook suggested the area to the north called the Bay of Islands would be suitable for settlement. The north of New Zealand is temperate and wet, while as one goes south the weather turns colder and drier.

Early settlement

The British viewed New Zealand as an offshoot of the Australian colony best used for whaling and sealing. Between 1820 and 1840 settlers began to pour into the country with or without crown permission. Most of the early settlement was promoted by real estate companies that sold land they often didn't own, together with passage and assistance to settlers. Edward Wakefield, while serving a prison sentence for abducting a schoolgirl heiress, devised the 'systematic colonization theory'. He formed the New Zealand Association, later called the New Zealand Company, to carefully select 'proper immigrants' dedicated to the formation of a classless egalitarian society. The profits from land sales were to fund free passage to New Zealand and to complete necessary public works before the settlers' arrival.

Although the idea wasn't bad, there were issues with execution. Thousands of settlers found themselves with no land, much less public works, which distressed the Maoris and the British government too. The British, after several bloody battles with the Maoris, settled land claims with the Maoris by the treaty of Waitangi in 1840. The settlers continued to ignore the treaty, resulting in Maori wars that lasted another 30 years, with continuing land claims and tensions to this day.

Relations with Maoris

The Maori population tended to increase faster than the European population, resulting in increasing demands for Maori participation in the mainstream economy and 'fairer' land settlements. The government has made concerted efforts towards cultural integration with some success. One indicator of success is that many New Zealanders think the government has gone too far to favor Maori concerns. Land claims issues between the invader and the invaded can only be settled in two ways. Either the victors go home – not likely – or the invaded accept some form of reparation. In the case of New Zealand, there's a genuine effort to reach an equitable solution, but no final settlement to date.

Gold and lamb

Further immigration was spurred by the discovery of gold and by the invention of the refrigerated cargo ship. The effect of gold is obvious, the impact of refrigeration is not so apparent. The ability to refrigerate lamb and mutton for long duration voyages effectively turned New Zealand into a lamb and sheep farm, with sheep specially bred to graze on steep terrain, to feed English workers during the industrial revolutions and the two world wars. Large-scale sheep farming, to a greater extent than gold, enabled New Zealand to became an efficient and mostly self-reliant country. This special relationship between lamb and prosperity lasted until the UK joined the European common market and could no longer continue favorable trade relations with New Zealand to the exclusion of the rest of Europe. After some hard times, New Zealand diversified its agricultural base, with farming remaining one of the more important economic activities.

New Zealand's political and social values

New Zealand became a dominion of the British Empire in 1907 and became independent in 1947. The egalitarian ideas of New Zealand's original settlers resulted in a nation that prizes economic equality as well as investment in social infrastructure. New Zealand is a leader in women's suffrage, social security, trade unionism, child care services and education. The country remains nuclear free and essentially has disbanded its armed forces. The theory is that New Zealand is too far away and too much trouble for anybody to bother with, and that Australia and/or the US would come to the rescue if need be.

New Zealand and Australia have a special relationship in that nationals of either country can work in either country without work permits. In many respects, citizenship in either country works for both. This is a nice benefit for those who move to New Zealand but feel limited by the small market and less entrepreneurial atmosphere than Australia.

New Zealand, like Canada and Australia, designs and re-designs its immigration policies to attract skills, capital and population. In addition, New Zealand looks for people that the authorities think will fit into the social fabric. This is a very subjective standard but a real New Zealand concern. If you fit in – i.e. you at least speak excellent English – you will find visa processing, by immigration standards, rather pleasant and rapid.

The basics

New Zealand requires a minimum investment of NZ$1,000,000 and a two-year holding period and uses a points based system to evaluate applicants. As alternative pathways to immigrate to New Zealand have become more difficult, the popularity of the investor program has increased. Applicants must speak a reasonable level of English and be under 85 years of age. The points system blends business experience with age and the investment amount. For example, a 35 year old would receive nine points for age, one point for investing NZ $1million and two points for four years' business experience. The pass mark is currently 12, but changes from time to time.

The points system

Applicants must score total points equal to, or greater than, the pass mark at the time of application, with a minimum of one point (for NZ$1,000,000) for investment funds.

Age	Points	Business experience	Points	Investment funds	Points
25 – 29 years	10	2 years	1	$1,000,000	1
30 – 34 years	9	4 years	2	$1,500,000	2
35 – 39 years	8	6 years	3	$2,000,000	3
40 – 44 years	6	8 years	4	$2,500,000	4
45 – 49 years	4	10 years	5	$3,000,000	5
50 – 54 years	2			$3,500,000	6
55 – 64 years	0			$4,000,000	7
65 – 74 years	-2			$4,500,000	8
75 – 84 years	-4			$5,000,000	9
				$5,500,000	10
				$6,000,000	11

Business experience

Other than money, the key requirement is business experience. The applicant must own 25% or more of the enterprise used as a basis for proving business experience and must have worked a minimum of 30 hours per week in the enterprise(s). Business experience may include management or supervisory experience, particularly when the applicant held senior management positions within substantial businesses. Choosing the enterprise to prove business experience is not always straightforward. In such cases applicants with experience as senior managers or executives may qualify.

What investment funds qualify for points

One must provide evidence of ownership and current fair market value of the net assets used to qualify for points for investment funds. Given recent concerns over money laundering and the like, the authorities often require evidence of how the applicant acquired their assets and that the level of asset ownership is consistent with the applicant's earning history. Assets must be owned by the applicant or jointly with a spouse, common law spouse or child. Assets acquired by borrowing are not allowed, although it is possible to claim for gifted funds so long as these were legally gifted and were originally earned lawfully.

Many accounting firms issue reports verifying net worth and business history in order to facilitate the visa petition. As in most things, a logical and well-crafted report will increase the likelihood of a successful outcome to the application.

Procedures

Upon passing the points test, language and good character requirements, the applicant must:

● Transfer the investment funds into New Zealand

● Prove the investment funds have been invested in New Zealand, in NZ$ in a profit seeking investment

● Provide a New Zealand contact address.

Listed shares, commercial property, purchase of a business, and interestingly, bank deposits all qualify. The investment funds can be held in several different investments but may not be used to purchase personal assets such as a home.

Applicants have 12 months from the date of approval to satisfy these conditions. Upon satisfaction of the conditions, all persons included in the application (spouse and children) must land in New Zealand, at which time they receive a multiple entry Returning Residence Visa (RRV) valid for two years.

The investment funds must remain invested in New Zealand for two years. Conditional status will be removed upon submitting proof of maintaining the required investment at the conclusion of the two years. At this time the applicant and family are issued life-long RRVs without any conditions.

Conclusion

Experienced business people with enough money can move to New Zealand simply by investing in the share market or buying a commercial property. I'm surprised more people don't do it. Economic opportunities are limited by the small population and remote location. The main reason to move to New Zealand is quality of life, which is fantastic and reasonably priced. The main disadvantage to living in New Zealand is location. Everywhere but Australia is a long way away. Please be aware that New Zealand immigration policies can change frequently and without advance notice and intending applicants must update themselves on the current policy before progressing their interest.

Acknowledgements

Mathew Collins, Frans Buysse and Richard Howard contributed to this article. Frans Buysse has been active in the field of migration since 1986. He started working as a consultant for the Dutch Emigration Centres and later became immigration officer for the Canadian Embassy. In 1993 he founded Buysse Immigration Consultancy, a team of professional consultants based in the Netherlands. He offers a full package of services to prospective immigrants to Australia, Canada, New Zealand and the United States of America.

Email: buysse@visaspecialist.com.

Mathew Collins is founder of Ambler Collins, one of Europe's oldest multi-destinational immigration consultancies. Ambler Collins maintains branch offices in London and Sydney.

Email: Mathew@amblercollins.com

Richard Howard is Managing Director of Pathways to New Zealand Ltd, a New Zealand-based specialist immigration consultancy established in 1992. PathwaysNZ focuses on investor and business visa applications, assisting with visa applications, and processing as well as locating appropriate investment opportunities in New Zealand. Website: www.pathwaysNZ.com Email: richard@pathwaysNZ.com

14 · South Africa

South Africa primarily caters to Europeans who buy flats to retire in Capetown or its environs. The Southern Cape offers unparalled scenic beauty, good food and wine and great weather in a modern cosmopolitain environment. Those who love wine, golf, fishing and sport in general will be thrilled. On top of that it's cheap. The negatives are that race relations are strained, and the government, if you need to access it, can be more frustrating than we are used to in Europe or North America. Quality medical care exists but one must do some homework to find it. The country as a whole offers beautiful scenery, great weather and fantastic opportunities to view the wild animals. As one goes north from the Cape, race relations deteriorate. The Cape is a European-friendly enclave, whereas the rest of the country, with few exceptions, suffers from squalor and high crime rates.

The government is a parliamentary democracy controlled by one political party, the ANC or African National Congress. The ANC replaced the Nationalist Party (Afrikaner) who installed aparthied and ran the country since 1948. Politics and voting patterns are still based on racial lines rather than on political principles. This means virtually all of the black electorate votes ANC. The ANC will be in power as long as they control the black vote.

In reality, South Africa has been a one-party state since 1948. The main difference between the Nationalists and the ANC is that the ANC includes some whites and other minorities and, while favoring black economic development, the ANC hasn't systematically oppressed the rest of the population as did the Nationalists. This is a big improvement. Despite complaints about ANC incompetence, things have improved for more people than under Nationalist rule. Furthermore, South Africa has been re-admitted to world culture and commerce. This is a huge improvement.

South Africa offers a business investor category that requires hiring locals, obtaining business plan approval and playing some role in the business. Other than to mention the program's existence, I won't elaborate because retirees and passive investors have other, easier, options.

Permanent residence

One may obtain permanent residence by being independently wealthy.

Applicants must:

● Provide certification by a chartered accountant of a minimum net worth of R 20,000,000

● Pay R 100,000 to the Department of Home Affairs

The applicant and spouse and children under the age of 21 also qualify.

Retirees of no specific age limit must provide a chartered accountant certification that they have:

● The right to a pension, *or*

● An irrevocable annuity, *or*

● A retirement account,

any of which will give them a minimum prescribed amount for the rest of their life

OR

● That the person concerned has a minimum prescribed net worth of not less than R 12,000,000 providing an income of at least R 20,000 per month.

Again, spouse and children under the age of 21 will qualify with the principal applicant.

None of the above categories permit outside employment.

All of the categories, except the last one prescribing a net worth of at least R12 million, allow the examiner great leeway in approving the petition. South Africa has some of the most passionate local politics concerning immigration in the world. I recommend avoiding as much as possible categories that rely upon local approval or an immigration examiner's definition of the minimum amount of income necessary for the rest of one's life.

Conclusion

Most people move to South Africa for a second home. The Cape area is one of the world's paradises for climate, quality food and wine and a vibrant international city. The more adventurous settle in other areas of the country, often to access game parks. These areas tend to be more dangerous from a crime point of view and less cosmopolitan. Housing is abundant and by European standards very reasonable. One can find very nice view apartments in the Capetown area for US$200,000. One of the biggest advantages is that you are a ten-hour flight, yes that's a long flight, to any major European city without jet lag. The lack of jet lag makes a huge difference in one's desire to go to South Africa more than once.

Acknowledgements

Special thanks to Mathew Collins of Ambler Collins based in London. Email: Mathew@amblercollins.com. Website: www. amblercollins.com

15 · Spain

Due to the geographic and cultural attractions in Spain, many United States citizens and other foreign nationals wish to retire or take an extended holiday in Spain. To encourage investment and business development, the Spanish immigration service does accommodate those foreigners who wish to take up residence in Spain but have no intention to work during their stay. The Spanish immigration service is a flexible, ever-changing system that lacks clear immigration procedures. Sometimes immigration matters are taken on a case-by-case basis.

This chapter will focus on the Spanish visa categories that allow an individual to remain in Spain for an extended stay without filing a work permit application – Residence Visa for Investors or Self-Employment and Residence Visas for Non-Lucrative Purposes.

Immigration policy

Spanish Immigration requires all persons (other than Spanish citizens, Spanish permanent residents and European Union citizens) who will be taking up gainful employment to obtain employment authorization prior to entering Spain, with limited exceptions. EU nationals are not required to obtain work permits, but are required to obtain a residence permit. However, this may change due to recent changes in EU regulations.

Non-EU citizens

Citizens of the US and visa exempt nationals are not required to obtain visas prior to entering Spain, but must indicate to the immigration officer in the Primary Inspection Line at the port of entry that they are coming to Spain as a business visitor. Business visitors cannot have intent to join the Spanish labor market. Their principal place of business and their primary remuneration source must be outside of Spain. Permissible business activities for a typical business visitor are business meetings, negotiations, business or professional conventions, consulting, research and soliciting of business.

Citizens who require a visa must obtain a Schengen visa or business visa prior to their arrival in Spain, from the Spanish consulate having jurisdiction over their place of residence. Business visitors and tourists will be admitted into Spain either for the duration of their temporary visit (as indicated in a corporate support letter) or for a maximum period of 90 days within a six-month period starting from the date of their first entry into Spain. However, if an employee is admitted to Spain under a visitor status, he or she may not be lawfully employable without first obtaining a work permit. This employee will not be able to change to employment status while in Spain. There are no extensions of the 90-day period unless there is an urgent reason, such as health or family emergency.

It is important to note that the 90-day time period is inclusive of all the Schengen territories which include: Austria, Belgium, Denmark, Finland, France, Germany, Greece, Iceland, Italy, Luxembourg, the Netherlands, Norway, Portugal, Spain and Sweden. Under the Schengen Agreement time is cumulative. Thus, if an individual went to Spain for two months starting February 1, 2004, then traveled to the United Kingdom, which is not part of the Schengen territories, for one month, he or she could return to Spain for one more month during the six-month period, or until July 31, 2004. However, if after spending two months in Spain, the individual spent the month of April in Germany, he or she would have capped-out the 90-day period and would not be able to return to Spain.

General visa qualifications and application procedures

There are two Spanish investment visas which allow for an individual to reside in Spain and not obtain the appropriate work visa. If you wish to invest in Spain, you will need to file either a Residence Visa for Non Lucrative Purposes or a Residence Visa for Investors or Self Employment. These Residence Visa applications must be filed at the Spanish consulate having jurisdiction over your place of residence.

Residence Visa for Non-Lucrative Purposes

If you wish to reside solely in Spain without working, an application for a Residence Visa for Non-Lucrative Purposes should be filed. You must demonstrate to the Spanish consulate that you have sufficient financial resources by providing financial statements, federal tax returns, investments and brokerage accounts. You must demonstrate an annual minimum income of US$75,000. Your stated income cannot be derived while working in Spain.

You must also provide evidence of citizenship, such as a valid passport. If you are in the US in a non-immigrant visa category, you must provide evidence of valid US immigration status such as an H-1B visa endorsed in the passport, a I-94 card, and an H-1B petition approval, I-797. You will need to provide two passport sized photographs and a government filing fee to process the application. The consulate generally will want to see proof of residency while in Spain such as a copy of a rental agreement, or proof of purchase of a home, i.e. a title or deed. Importantly, the consulate will want to see proof of medical insurance while in Spain. The consulate also requires a medical certificate confirming that you are free of addictions and mental illness and have been vaccinated for the following: yellow fever, cholera and the plague. In addition, you must provide a police certificate of good conduct from your local police precinct. This must be done for each city you have resided in for more than six months for the past five years. Lastly, all the documents discussed above must be translated into Spanish and may require either legalizations or *apostilles*. Upon receipt of the visa application at the Spanish consulate, the processing time is approximately five months but may exceed this timeframe.

Residence Visa for Investor or Self-Employed

If you want to reside in Spain and be self-employed or work at a company in which you invest the requisite capital, you must file a Residence Visa for Investor or Self Employed. You must first file a work permit application with the Ministry of Labor. The Ministry of Labor then issues a *Solicitud e Permiso de Trabajo* that must be filed with the Spanish consulate within 30 days of the date stamped on the approval. If the *Solicitud e Permiso de Trabajo* is not filed within this timeframe, the approval is rendered void.

You must then file a Residence Visa application form at the consulate, along with supporting documentation. You must provide evidence of citizenship, such as a valid passport. If you are in the US in a non-immigrant visa category, you must provide evidence of valid US immigration status such as an H-1B visa endorsed in the passport, a I-94 card, and an H-1B petition approval, I-797. You will need to provide two passport sized photographs and a government filing fee to process the application. The consulate generally will want to see proof of residency while in Spain such as a copy of a rental agreement, or proof of purchase of a home, i.e. a title or deed.

The consulate requires proof of medical insurance while in Spain. The consulate also requires a medical certificate confirming that you are free of addictions and mental illness and have been vaccinated for the following: yellow fever, cholera and the plague. The doctor must expressly state in the medical certificate that the individual, 'does not have evidence of any health conditions which would prevent the applicant from engaging in the proposed activity in Spain.' In addition, you must provide a police certificate of good conduct from your local police precinct. This must be done for each city you have resided in for more than six months for the past five years. Lastly, all the documents discussed above must be translated into Spanish and may require either legalizations or *Apostilles*. Upon receipt of the Residence Visa for Non-Lucrative Purposes application at the Spanish Consulate, the processing time is approximately four months but may exceed this timeframe.

Residence card

Once you arrive in Spain with your Residence Visa for Investors or Self Employment or Residence Visa for Non Lucrative purposes, you must apply at the local police precinct for a Spanish Residence Card. This process takes approximately one month and you must provide an original passport containing an endorsed Residence Visa, medical report(s), police certificate(s), marriage and birth certificate(s), all of which should have been legalized at the Spanish Consulate General.

Dependents filed at the Spanish consulate

Generally, your spouse and unmarried dependent children are included on your visa application at the Spanish consulate. A personal appearance may be required by the Spanish consulate for each family member and is discretionary. Spouses must find their own independent employer if they wish to work while residing in Spain.

Conclusion

As Spanish Immigration is not always straightforward, additional documentation may be requested throughout the process. It is imperative that you provide complete and thorough visa applications. If you do not provide sufficient supporting documentation, your application may be denied, potentially resulting in significant hardship to yourself and accompanying family members. An individual entering Spain for a short business trip or for employment must be in lawful immigration status. You should never enter as a tourist when you are representing a company.

Although historically there has been little enforcement of Spanish immigration regulations, the climate is changing throughout the world, and we can expect to see further changes in Spain. You are advised to comply strictly with the law in order to avoid damaging consequences to both yourself and accompanying family members.

Acknowledgements

Deborah B. Davy manages the Global Visa Group specializing in global visas and global compliance at Berry, Appleman & Leiden. She is skilled at managing high-volume international personnel transfers, both for short-term and long-term assignments, for large multinational companies in the high technology, manufacturing and financial sectors. She specializes in assisting global corporations in designing, developing and implementing successful international visa programs. Ms Davy has established strong working relationships with the premier service providers worldwide and has an encyclopedic knowledge of the rules and procedures associated with global visa and work permit processes. Ms Davy received her J.D. from Thomas Jefferson School of Law and was admitted to the California Bar in 1997. She was Law Review Editor-in-Chief of the San Diego Justice Journal. She competed in the Phillip C. Jessup International Moot Court Competition. She is a member of American Immigration Lawyers Association and is a frequent speaker on global visa practice issues.

16 · Switzerland

Switzerland has a reputation of being closed to immigrants. This is far from the truth. A quick visit would indicate that the percentage of foreign population is probably higher than that of the USA or Canada. In fact, this would be true of most Northern European countries. Switzerland's central location in Europe, superior medical system, lack of wealth envy, track record of avoiding wars and invasion, excellent educational system and general quality of life, attracts retirees and persons of independent means from all over the world.

The Swiss system generally requires applicants first to obtain permission from the canton (region) and then qualify under the federal standards. One must demonstrate local ties or a job creating financial commitment. There's one set of lax rules for European Union (EU) citizens and another set of rules for everybody else.

Non-EU investor

The preferred route for people from outside the EU who are under 55 years of age is to invest at least Sfr 500,000 in a small or medium size company in the canton where you want to live. The investment may be debt, equity or a combination and must finance the growth of an active trade or business with employees. Passive investments in real estate or bank accounts do not qualify. A qualifying investment must be maintained as long as you live in Switzerland.

You must be retired with no active employment in Switzerland and limited activities outside of Switzerland. You must have an annual income of at least Sfr100,000 per year and make Switzerland your permanent residence, i.e. six months per year. There are 'case by case exceptions' to the residency rules. The visa includes spouses and children under 18 years of age, who may not work. The visa permits you to buy Swiss real estate, which isn't freely traded as in the English-speaking countries, and you may elect to pay tax under the lump sum tax system. Basically, one must be financially self-sufficient.

The lump sum tax system exempts investors from income tax and instead levies an annual lump sum payment based on one's rental expenditures in Switzerland. For example, a person with annual rental expenditure of Sfr 36,000 would pay a tax equal to Sfr 36,000 × 5 × 30% or Sfr 54,000. If you own a residence, the tax authorities create an imputed rent based on the home's value to do the calculation.

Here's the kickers. The visa is only valid for a year and must be renewed annually. Not every canton offers the program. The canton can reject applicants for purely subjective reasons. Unless you are famous, you need to show previous ties to Switzerland such as frequent trips, friends or relatives. It's something like joining a fraternal order or club on a year-by-year basis. If you do qualify, citizenship takes about 12 years and is also a very subjective process.

Non-EU retiree

Non-EU citizens over 55 years of age may qualify for a retirement visa if they have no day-to-day job responsibilities, live in Switzerland for six months or more a year, have an annual income of Sfr 100,000 or more, and can demonstrate ties to Switzerland. The process and procedures are similar to the investor visa described above except that the emphasis is on ties to Switzerland, i.e., whether they want you, as opposed to making a specific investment.

EU-citizens

EU 15 (referring to the 15 EU countries that were members before 2004) 'retirees' and persons of 'independent means' may qualify with as little as Sfr 50,000 annual income and receive a five-year permit that includes spouse, children under 18 years of age and financially dependent parents. Applicants may not work in Switzerland and are restricted to working in part-time capacities abroad such as being on a board of directors, writing or consulting. There is no age limit for this visa. Applicants must demonstrate independent means to support their family and may not access social assistance. Unlike the non-EU investor category, EU applicants may live and buy real estate where they wish. They are not tied to living in a particular canton. Retirees must make Switzerland their permanent residence and may elect lump sum taxation (see above).

Conclusion

To summarize, it's relatively easy to obtain the type of residence status that would enable one to take advantage of the Swiss quality of life. In other words, if you want to ski and hike, financially qualified persons shouldn't have much problem. Things become much more difficult and dependent on local contacts for those who wish to make Switzerland their primary residence and to become integrated into Swiss society in terms of rights to purchase land and seek employment. Switzerland is not open to immigrants in a manner similar to Australia or Canada, but will accept financially qualified persons who demonstrate they do not need to rely on local services, funds or employment.

17 · Thailand

Thailand, located in the center of South East Asia, offers tropical beaches, a spring-like tropical mountain climate in the north, particularly Changmai, and an interesting local culture. The countryside and beaches are simply beautiful. Thailand gets good or bad press, depending on your point of view, for whoring and boozing tours. The sex trade certainly exists and even flourishes, but there is much more to Thailand than sex tours. The economy is varied and vibrant, offering interesting investment and business opportunities to those so inclined.

Many foreigners have settled in Changmai because of its temperate climate and more reasonable pace of life. Bangkok is a huge sprawling city that can be a lot of work to negotiate, particularly on a daily basis. There is a large ex-pat community from all over the world. Telephone, email and all the modern conveniences are readily available and housing is very reasonably priced and of high standard. The rest of the country is generally hot and hotter. One can tour a variety of temples, wats and ancient ruins. There are tropical mountain hikes and Mekong River boat trips through a national park that includes the infamous Golden Triangle.

Some 25 years ago, a friend and I hiked from Chang Rai, a northern town, into the jungle. We came upon a village run by a Chinese bandit involved in the heroin trade. The village was heavily armed and was quite surprised to see two unarmed Americans strolling down main street. My companion spoke Thai and explained we were simply trekking. The head man treated us to a meal of stewed dog, the local meat staple, and sent us on our way. This area is now in a national park. Times change.

Thailand managed to keep its independence during the colonial period. This makes a bigger difference than one might think. Basically the locals, although protective of their culture, don't have a chip on their shoulder toward westerners. The government is stable, in a way. Military and civilian coups occur with more regularity than one would like but they generally aren't violent or disruptive. The King, a constitutional monarch with more direct powers and arguably more moral persuasion than the Queen of England, inevitably intercedes to keep things civil. It's a crime to bad mouth the King – one intermittently reads about an unfortunate foreigner who said the wrong thing and ended up in jail.

Visa programs

Thailand, due to popular demand, finally offers a retirement visa. Permanent residence visa approval depends on the vetting of investment projects through industry and government panels and in most cases, requires a local joint venture partner. Due to the complexity of local politics and the cumbersome procedures, few people avail themselves of the immigrant investor categories.

The non-immigrant category, discussed below, simply requires a bank deposit, proof of sufficient assets and good moral standing. This category is widely used by people who wish to live in Thailand for lifestyle reasons. Permanent residence through investment is, although reasonably priced, subject to restrictive social policy and subjective regulations. On one hand, Thailand wants to open its economy; on the other, it's the only country in the region that was never colonized and is protective, rightly so, of its culture.

Permanent residence through investment

A foreign investor or retiree qualifies to apply for a residence permit after a period of three years of residency immediately prior to the date of application. Retirees must be at least 60 years old with a net monthly income no less than 30,000 baht.

A board (BOI) vets investment proposals for intending permanent residents. In addition to vetting the investment proposal, the board may vet the character of the applicant. For retirees or investors, the relevant program requires a direct investment of a minimum of 10 million baht in a new project that either is eligible for investment promotion under the Investment Promotion Act or which meets the criteria set forth by the Committee for Granting Permanent Residence. In most cases, the applicant must bring in funds to invest in a new project that has not started operations. Alternatively, investors may purchase a condominium or designated securities.

If the project is not eligible for investment promotion by the BOI, the project must benefit the country in the following ways:

● Produce for export

● Increase employment

● Utilize indigenous raw materials

● Locate in provincial areas

● Encourage technology transfer to Thai nationals

Projects may not:

● Compete in such a way as to destroy existing domestic businesses

● Hinder the growth of existing domestic businesses, or domestic businesses which have not yet been developed

The investment must be in a joint venture of a newly or already established company. The joint venture must generally include Thai nationals. The applicant must hold more than 25% of the registered capital, unless the size of the project exceeds 100 million baht, excluding the cost of land and working capital. In that case, the shareholding criteria may be relaxed. The applicant must maintain the investment for at least three years from the date permanent residence is granted.

Applicants may apply for permanent residence for the following family members:

● Spouse

● Parents

● Not more than three children who are unmarried and under 20 years old.

Note that Thailand limits the application to three children.

Retirees may also invest in securities designated by the Ministry of Finance and the Bank of Thailand or buy a condominium. The investment thresholds are:

● 8 Million baht for the investor

● 6 million baht for a spouse

● 2 million baht per unmarried child under the age of 20

Investors must hold the bonds or property for five years and may not use them as collateral for a loan. The investment must also be approved by the Board of Investments, which considers the applicant's overall financial situation as well.

Most permanent residence retirees simply buy a condominium apartment. It is the easiest of the alternatives and you need to live somewhere anyway. Investing in a business requires Committee approval, which involves politics. The caveats on investing in a business mean you need a local partner. In short, you won't qualify unless somebody local wants you as a partner.

Temporary residence

Temporary residence permits valid for one year are another story. Investors may simply bring more than 3 million baht to Thailand for one year of residence. Under current rules, one can extend year by year as long as the 3 million baht stays in Thailand.

To qualify:

1. The applicant must show that three million baht has been transferred in their name to any bank in Thailand.

2. The transfer of money must be:

   ● Fixed deposit in any government bank

   ● Purchase of government bonds

   ● Purchase of a condominium

   ● Other investments that the Office of Immigration Bureau considers beneficial to the country

3. Applicants may combine investments as long as the total is at least three million baht.

4. The Office of Immigration Bureau reserves the right to terminate the stay of the investors in the Kingdom if they fail to inform the Office of Immigration Bureau in advance of a change of their investment activities.

The non-immigrant retiree (temporary residence) visa is much easier to deal with and will be sufficient for most western retirees. Frankly, most long-term western residents are men who obtain permanent residence through marriage rather than investment. Rather than go through investment boards, local partners and politics, it's much easier to buy a condominium or make a three million baht bank deposit.

Conclusion

Many foreigners thoroughly enjoy life in Thailand. The people are very friendly and polite and welcoming of foreigners as long as the foreigners don't involve themselves in politics or politically sensitive businesses. If you are happy simply enjoying life in Thailand, it can be great and the people are generally wonderful. If you want to become involved in Thai culture and politics, become a Thai and get involved in the upper echelons of society, things will be more difficult and most Thais will wonder why you have to come to Thailand to get involved rather than staying home where you belong. Modern communications and excellent air connections make it easy to leave when necessary. The bureaucracy can be slow and frustrating but things get done. It's best to go with the flow because you aren't going to change the way things are done in Thailand.

18 · United Kingdom

Who moves to the UK and why? Most people visualize the British as a people in a rush to leave their island. The truth is that the UK is one of the world's most sought after immigration destinations. The UK attracts skilled workers worldwide and many Commonwealth residents moved to the UK as the colonies achieved independence.

Since this book is about investment immigration not tied to employment, we'll focus on that segment of the world's population. This upper crust of humanity comes to the UK for culture, London night life, shows, theatre, life in a country estate, golf, access to Europe without having to live in Europe where the legal system and language differs, access to the vibrant financial life of London and more. Simply put, there is a market for what is perceived as an English upper class lifestyle. Understanding this market, the authorities created a visa category tailored to people of means who simply wish to live in the UK without reliance on local employment.

Postcard from the UK about our investor program

By Roger Gherson of Gherson & Co, immigration solicitors based in London, Email: info@gherson.com, roger@gherson.com

The UK currently offers one of the most thoughtful immigration policies in the world. The UK's Managed Migration policy encourages significant numbers of both long-term and short-term economic migrants. This presently numbers about 200,000 a year and includes smaller numbers of entrepreneurs and investors. Most countries either do not see any importance in inward migration, or they develop their policies in a piecemeal and disjointed way, just reacting to economic and political events as they occur. The UK understands that it needs to reverse the brain drain to prosper.

The most exciting program under the Managed Migration umbrella is the Highly Skilled Migrant Program (HSMP), which enables people to come for employment or self-employment if they pass an objective assessment of whether they are likely to succeed. Also useful is the Innovator category, making it easy for persons with business acumen to migrate.

Turning specifically to the UK's Investor category, the basic program dates back to 1 October 1994. The program required the applicant to transfer £1 million to the UK – a substantial investment as immigrant investor programs go, especially ten years ago. The program's expense may explain a meager annual uptake in double figures.

The Managed Migration policy not only created new programs like HSMP and Innovator, but also overhauled many pre-existing programs. The Investor rules were reviewed and amended with effect from 13 January 2004. The UK authorities hope the changes will encourage more high net worth individuals to move to the UK.

The UK Immigrants Investor program – the basic rules

Basically, the investor must bring at least £1 million to the UK and must invest at least £750,000 of it in specified types of investment. Before 13 January 2004, the £1 million had to be the investor's own money, but now investors with a world wide net worth of at least £2 million may borrow up to £1 million in the UK from financial institutions regulated by the Financial Services Authority. The new rules allow high net worth individuals to rely on funds borrowed in the UK against their wealth elsewhere.

The specified investment of £750,000 includes investments in government bonds, or active and trading UK registered companies. These companies may be listed or private. One may create a portfolio of shares, unit trusts, etc., and/or invest in one or more private businesses. The investment risks range from the safety of government bonds to investments in speculative high tech ventures. Passive investments in real estate do not qualify. Real estate development and businesses with real property as a major asset – e.g. a hotel business – may qualify. Investments may include debt arrangements, secured or unsecured, where it can be proved that a UK company benefited from the loan.

Originally, the investor program was designed to attract entrepreneurial skills as well as investment capital. To this end, investors may take up self-employment in the UK. Ten years later, there is certainly no *expectation* that the investor will be an active entrepreneur. The HSMP and Innovator programs more readily accommodate such persons; no investment required.

Lack of clear goals

The new program, while certainly inviting and flexible, lacks an over-riding philosophy. Is the UK government looking for some level of risk taking, or entrepreneurship, or simply the money? Immigrant investor programs need an over-riding philosophy and clear social purpose to withstand political vagaries and to give investors and those marketing the program some assurance that they can rely upon a set of consistent rules for a reasonable period of time. Without clear goals, there is no way to measure the program's effectiveness. This only empowers those who are against investment immigration to find ways to kill the program.

Several inconsistencies immediately become apparent. The UK program prevents applicants from merely making a bank deposit or purchasing property to qualify. Bank deposits benefit the economy in the same way as a purchase of government bonds and carry more risk. Property investments require several ancillary trades and services which arguably provide greater economic impact than the purchase of a corporate or government bond and carry more risk. The purchase of publicly traded securities, other than the initial offering, merely represents a bet between the purchaser and seller on the future of the security. The company that issued the security has no benefit from this transaction. If this program is to survive, the UK authorities need to clarify the benefits they wish the program to produce.

Other requirements

Unlike with the US program, applicants do not have to transfer funds to the UK before applying. Applicants need to satisfy the authorities that they have the funds and the intention to transfer the appropriate capital to the UK (or raise it there) shortly after arriving in the UK with Investor status.

Applicants must demonstrate sufficient funds to support themselves without recourse to employment (though an investor may establish or join a business or work in self-employment, e.g. as a consultant). Applicants must also demonstrate they will not use public funds – i.e., state assistance. This does *not* prevent use of the UK's National Health Service or state education. Spouses and unmarried children under 18 years of age may accompany the applicant and seek any employment.

The applicant must intend to make the UK a 'main home'. This generally means spending no more than 25–30% of the time outside the UK. While there is discretion to be more flexible, this is an issue. Most people who possess the amount of money required to move to the UK will not want to be tied to spending 70% of their time in one place.

Tax liability

The residency requirements in practice mean that applicants must subject themselves to some, not all, UK taxation. It means being liable in respect of income remitted into the UK mainland and income arising in the UK (e.g. from self-employment or dividends from the mandatory investment). The UK tax system offers some flexibility in that non-domiciled individuals do not pay tax on a world-wide basis, only on income remitted into the mainland or arising here. 'Domicile' for UK tax purposes does not mean the same thing as 'permanent residence' for immigration purposes. For example, one may maintain a closer connection with one's home country for tax purposes and at the same time hold UK permanent residence status for immigration purposes. With careful planning, one may be non-domiciled for tax purposes as well as permanent resident for immigration purposes.

Obtaining permanent residence

Investor status initially confers a one-year conditional period. At the end of the one-year period, investors may apply for an additional three years if the applicant verifies the required investment of £750,000, that overall £1 million or more has been brought to (or raised in) the UK, and that the other requirements are satisfied. After a total of four years in the UK with Investor status, the applicant and family members may apply for permanent residence, technically known as 'indefinite leave to remain' or 'settlement'. Regular absences from the UK for six months in any given year generally breaks the continuity of the four-year period.

Making the application

Generally applicants under the Investor program must apply from abroad, in person, before an entry clearance officer (ECO) at a British Consular post. The ECO is not empowered to make decisions and simply clarifies the application before sending the papers and interview notes to the Home Office in the UK. Exceptions occur where applicants already in the UK clearly satisfy the substantive requirements.

HSBC capital

HSBC Capital offers an innovative solution for those wishing to avail themselves of the UK investor visa program. Simply put and by way of example only, the applicant makes a down payment of £100,000 and HSBC loans the applicant £900,000. The proceeds are used to purchase a variety of securities and bonds. The investor loses the investment income and £100,000 down payment, which is used to pay loan interest, commissions and fees. HSBC generally refers applicants to outside legal counsel for immigration petition preparation and advice. The actual terms and conditions depend on prevailing interest rates and investor financial qualifications. Below is a description of the HSBC loan program written by Eric Major, Vice President of HSBC Capital (Canada) Inc.

Background

HSBC Capital (Canada) Inc. ('HCCA') has been actively promoting the Canadian Immigrant Investor program since 1991 and has assisted over 2,500 investors and their families in immigrating to Canada. It has developed an expertise in the specialized area of immigration to Canada via the Investor category. It has established an extensive network of business introducers in key locations around the world, and leverages-off the bank's impressive global office network to source potential immigrant investors (HCCA is a member of HSBC Group). HSBC Group is one of the world's largest banking and financial services organizations, with over 9,500 offices in 79 countries and territories. It also has a comprehensive website (www.hsbc.ca/iip) that sources 20% of its investor clientele.

HCCA started investigating the UK immigration rules in early 2002 as a result of some of its customers expressing a preference in immigrating to the UK over Canada. In particular, with its experience in the Canadian Immigrant Investor program, HCCA considered the UK Immigrant Investor program in detail and saw an opportunity to design a package of services to support high net worth ('HNW') individuals seeking to immigrate to the UK. Over the last 18 months, HCCA has informally researched market interest from HNW individuals based around a package of services tailored to assist them once they decide to immigrate to the UK.

The new UK investor program

Prior to 13 January 2004, the UK Investor program had attracted a relatively small number of individuals (less than 50 applications each year). The program's immigration rules were silent on one key feature, namely, the ability to finance the investment. HCCA's discussions with potential immigrants indicated that the program would be more attractive to HNW individuals if they were permitted to finance the £1 million investment. Prospective migrants are often entrepreneurs reluctant to tie up their capital or liquidate existing investments. They often prefer to take advantage of sophisticated banking and investment products to leverage the maximum opportunity from their existing wealth. Therefore, the ability to make the UK investment via a loan was seen as a key enhancement to the UK Investor program, as it enables the individual to leverage their wealth more effectively, freeing up their capital for other personal and business uses.

As a result of these conclusions, HCCA held discussions with the Immigration and Nationality Directorate (IND) throughout 2002 and 2003 to discuss possible amendments to the existing program. A proposal was made in October 2002 for the IND to consider revising the Investor category rules to allow financing. After a number of further discussions, potential parameters were submitted to the IND in June 2003. In September 2003, the then UK Immigration Minister, Beverley Hughes MP, advised that the proposals had been agreed in broad terms. In concurrence with our proposal, the UK government does not wish to dilute the calibre of individuals that this program seeks to attract to the UK, and so the amended rules will be targeted at individuals with **net**

assets exceeding £2 million, and will run alongside the existing scheme as part of the overall program. The program enhancements were announced by Minister Hughes at the International Bar Association's Global Business Immigration Conference in London on 20 November 2003. The rules were subsequently amended and published on 13 January 2004.

The HSBC 'all inclusive' service proposal

The 'All Inclusive' service offers HNW individuals a package of services tailored to assist them once they decide to immigrate to the UK (similar to a service package currently offered by HCCA under the Canadian Immigrant Investor program).

The combined offering provides a number of benefits for an all-inclusive fee of approximately £100,000. These include:

● Easy access to professional immigration advice via specialist immigration lawyers to ensure client understanding of the UK's requirements and the relative advantages/disadvantages of the various immigration categories available to the client.

● Efficient administration of all immigration formalities and paperwork on behalf of the client, including referral to outside legal counsel.

● Production of a Background Verification Report to support their immigration application.

● Initial tax and financial planning advice, making recommendations prior to establishing residence in the UK.

● Access to the full range of private banking services through a dedicated relationship manager.

● The four-year financing cost for a loan that is designed to assist the client in meeting the investment requirement under the UK Investor Program.

● Effortless introductions to specialist services such as Property Vision, insurance, etc.

HCCA's experience in this field shows that HNW individuals prefer to approach a single, reputable and trustworthy institution to assist them with the complexities associated with immigrating to a new country. There are many practical and emotional issues involved in moving one's family to a new country and so the ability to provide a 'one-stop-shop' to HNW individuals is key. The HSBC service proposal will assist the potential immigrant in:

- Satisfying the £1 million investment requirement under the program
- Meeting all of the government and legal requirements under the selected program
- Addressing the tax implications of moving to the UK
- Satisfying their banking and financial needs upon their arrival
- Considering real-estate opportunities in the Greater London area, through Property Vision
- Assisting them in developing a network of local professionals and cultural support groups.

Pros and cons

Pros

- **Quick processing** If the file is properly prepared, the IND can normally provide a decision within four weeks.
- **No business experience required** For example, an applicant can be a housewife joining her children while they are studying in England. By investing under this program, she can yield 'indefinite leave to remain' (ILR) for the entire family.
- **Affordable** Through financing, ILR can be achieved for an all-in cost of only £100,000 (as long as the applicant and spouse have a personal net worth exceeding £2 million).
- **Favourable tax treatment** Most immigrant investors under this program will be deemed Residents/Non-Domicile for tax purposes, enabling significant tax advantages (i.e. shelter worldwide income).
- **For the children** Access to the entire EU for work and education.

- **Citizenship** Attainable within five years, as long as they meet the stringent residency requirements (below).

Cons

- Strict residency requirements: the main applicant **must** spend most of their time in the UK for at least four years in order to obtain ILR, and for at least five years in order to attain citizenship.

- Unlike Canada, which provides immediate 'Permanent Residence' status upon approval, the UK Immigrant Investor Program provides temporary status for the initial four years, until ILR can be obtained.

Conclusion

If you have enough money, the British have made it as easy as any country in the world to achieve immigration status. It's as simple as buying a home and buying traded securities that you might have purchased anyway. As a rule, visa processing is fast and efficient by immigration standards. Immigration bureaucracies worldwide are notoriously high-handed and inefficient. This is much less so in the case of the UK. Probably the biggest thing to make sure you have handled is taxation. The concept of living in a jurisdiction as a permanent resident, and claiming exemption from worldwide taxation, presents an obvious contradiction and therefore requires careful advance planning.

19 · United States

The USA stretches from the Atlantic to the Pacific Oceans and includes virtually all of the world's climates and land forms, as well as controversial presidents. It takes about 36 hours to drive from coast to coast non-stop. A drive from Seattle to Fairbanks, Alaska takes a similar amount of time. Culture, language, accents, politics and food vary from region to region. Housing costs and public education vary state by state. Each state has its own tax system. Before moving to the USA, one should take a driving tour to get the lay of the land. Life in California is not the same as life in Georgia. Depending on one's taste, it's better or worse but definitely different. Most immigrants settle in Florida and California with Florida being the more popular. The weather is warm in both places and housing in Florida is very reasonably priced.

Most people come from countries where political life is dominated by a strong central government. The USA also has a strong central government but most people have more interaction with city, county and state government. For example, state governments generally control public education. Municipal governments often control sewer, water, electricity, etc. In most areas, other than obvious things like defense spending, the Federal government lets the state governments manage local affairs. There are, of course, many over-riding Federal rules and programs but as a very general proposition, state, county and municipal governments manage local affairs.

The USA does not have a publicly funded health care system as is common in Europe. Medicare, which is publicly funded, covers medical costs for US citizens over 62 years of age. Medicare covers permanent residents to a lesser degree. Coverage percentages vary state by state. People under 62 require private insurance, normally provided by an employer. Since immigrant investors generally won't have an employer, they will need to purchase insurance packages from companies that cater to non-citizens. Such coverage can be expensive, say $1500 per person per month, but still cheaper than the taxes you paid for coverage back home. Many people purchase major medical insurance that only covers the big ones, i.e. cancer, heart attack, etc. This coverage tends to be much cheaper but you will need to pay for cuts, bruises, minor surgery, etc., yourself. States regulate insurance companies so private insurance packages vary state by state.

The USA has Federal tax, state tax and local tax. State income taxes are deductable from Federal income tax. State taxes range from next to nothing to as high as some countries. New York and California are notoriously high tax jurisdictions. Only four states have no personal income tax. Florida, Alaska and Washington State are three of them. The USA taxes world-wide income from all sources. The only ways to avoid worldwide income tax are to move all of your assets to the USA or transfer your assets to an offshore trust prior to moving to the USA. The trust avenue has some risks, in that the Internal Revenue Service (IRS) can ignore the trust if they believe it was set up in connection with becoming a permanent resident. To give an idea of the tax burden, a person with $200,000 in taxable income will generally pay 30% or $60,000 in Federal taxes. The actual amount depends on one's circumstances.

Contributing authors:

Lincoln Stone of Fainsbert, Mase and Snyder LLP, based in Los Angeles, California, lstone@fms-law.com. Mr. Stone is a recognized authority on the US immigrant investor program. Some of the information contained in this chapter came from articles authored by Mr. Stone.

Henry Liebman, President of American Life Inc., formerly Chairman of the Board of Northwest Business Bank, practised immigration law for some 20 years but now is focusing on business affairs. Mr. Liebman manages a regional center located in Seattle, Washington.

Climate and geography

Rather than describe cities and human-made land marks I here describe topography and climate, as an overall 'lay of the land' makes it easier to find a compatible climate and topography. I've driven across the USA at least ten times, taking a different route each trip. The following description is my view, not that of National Geographic or AAA (Automobile Association of America). I've summarized and generalized while attempting to describe the flavor of the terrain.

Latitude compared to Europe

As a rule the USA ranges from 23 degrees south to 48 degrees north. Western Europe, situated much further north than the USA, ranges from 35 degrees to 60 degrees, with Nordic countries extending north of the 60th parallel. The west coast of Europe tends to have mild wet weather while the East Coast of the USA, much farther south, has hot muggy summers and colder winters. The West Coast of the USA has similar weather to the west coast of Europe. The weather of Seattle, Washington, (on the 47th parallel) is very similar to the weather one finds in the Atlantic coastal regions of France at a similar latitude.

New York City and Madrid are both located a bit above 40 degrees north. New York's beaches are empty during the winter whereas Portuguese beaches at the same latitude are winter holiday destinations. The English settlers arriving at the Jamestown colony in Virginia mistakenly thought they would be coming to a Spanish climate, and the colony perished after the first winter.

The East Coast

Florida is flat as a pancake, with a climate ranging from tropical in the very south, and mild winters with hot and humid summers as one goes north. A coastal plain of varying width but usually no more than 100 miles wide runs from Georgia, north to New England. The summers remain hot and muggy, while the winters get progressively colder as one heads north.

Moving west from most points on the East Coast one encounters the Appalachian mountain range. This heavily forested range, basically high hills with a few peaks of 5,000 feet, runs from Georgia to Canada. Traversing the Appalachians one finds a vast deciduous woodland drained by the Mississippi River. Most cities in this region command strategic locations on the Mississippi River or its tributaries or on the Great Lakes.

The Great Lakes

The Great Lakes, located in the northern Midwest on the Canadian border, form an interconnected freshwater inland sea with access to the Atlantic Ocean through the St. Lawrence River and seaway. Lake

Michigan, not even the largest of the Great Lakes, is significantly larger than the country of Israel. The Great Lakes were extremely polluted for many years. The joke was that the water would instantly develop camera film. Now the salmon fishery attracts anglers from all over the world.

Inland from the East Coast

As one approaches the interior the climate tends to produce hotter summers, though still muggy, and colder winters often with large snowfalls. Many people prefer a genuinely hot summer and a definite change of seasons to the milder weather and less pronounced change of seasons one finds on the West Coast. The forests ranging from the Atlantic Ocean to the Mississippi river tend to be made up primarily of deciduous trees, such as oak, maple, cherry and birch. The forests in the far west tend to be conifers, such as pine, redwoods and Douglas fir.

Crossing the Mississippi River the woodlands soon disappear, turning into a vast prairie or sea of grass that extends to the Rocky Mountains. One of the better trout fly-fishing holes is the Gates of the Mountains, named by Lewis and Clark, where the Missouri River tumbles out of the Rocky Mountains to reach the great plains. Traversing the Great Plains from south to north the moisture content increases slightly and the winters become progressively colder. The original settlers lived in semi-underground sod huts to protect against high winds and cold. This is where the buffalo roamed. The modern landscape has more to do with corn and cows than buffalo. In fact you will see more buffalo on your menu than on the prairie.

The Rocky Mountains

The Rocky Mountains run from north to south through the entire country. It's basically the same range that starts in Tierra del Fuego and ends in the Alaskan Arctic. The tallest peaks, mostly located in Colorado, exceed 14,000 feet. If you want to be governor of Colorado you need to claim that you have climbed all or most of the peaks that exceed 14,000 feet. The mountain climate tends be warm and dry in the summer and cold and snowy in the winter. Many people enjoy the mountain climate, which is why Colorado and New Mexico have among the highest population growth rates in the USA.

The Great Basin

The region between the Rockies and the next mountain range, the Sierras in California, and the Cascades in Oregon to the south of the Columbia River, was known to the early explorers as the Great Basin. The Great Basin includes the Great Salt Lake, originally settled by Mormons fleeing persecution in the east, the deserts of Arizona and California, as well as the high desert of Eastern Washington and Eastern Oregon. The Spanish and succeeding explorers believed the Great Basin was drained by the Buenaventura River which crossed the Sierras and provided river passage to the Pacific in California. It turned out that the Columbia River, which starts in the Canadian Rockies, crosses the Cascade Mountains between the states of Washington and Oregon and reaches the sea at Astoria, Oregon, so the Buenaventura was wishful thinking.

A modern view of the Great Basin includes the golf courses of Arizona and Palm Springs, the Grand Canyon and the canyon national parks of Southern Utah, the golf courses of Bend, Oregon, some population along the western edge of the Rockies, the populous Great Salt Lake area of Utah, lots of agriculture and high desert. This is a vast region with many beautiful and uncrowded places to visit, fish, hike or golf. The Great Basin is semi-arid but drained by several rivers. The climate, always dry, varies depending on the position of surrounding mountains. St. George, Utah and Las Vegas have mild winters, and year-round golf. To the north, in Idaho, the winters can get quite cold.

Across the Sierras and the Cascades

Continuing to the west, we cross the Sierras in California and the Cascades further north. This long range of mountains separates the Great Basin from the Pacific. Active volcanoes punctuate these mountains. Mt. St. Helens blew while I was studying for the Law Bar Exams in 1980 and again in September of 2004. I climbed Mt. St. Helens – then 9,400 feet, now about 7,000 feet high – several times. Steam issued from glacial ice which vibrated under one's feet. In 1980 volcanic ash covered much of the states of Washington, Oregon, Idaho and Montana for several weeks.

The West Coast

Once in the coastal plain and the lower coastal mountains, the climate changes from Mediterranean in the south to maritime, cool and wet, as one proceeds north, much like moving from Spain, through France and then to the UK. The coastal areas include the coastal deserts of southern California, giant redwoods in northern California and the Pacific Northwest rainforest with its giant Douglas firs. Modern Los Angeles was originally a desert oasis. The Pacific northwest of the USA is known as the Persian Gulf of trees. One often sees 150 ft high Douglas firs in suburban Washington and Oregon cities.

California is one of the largest economies in the world and the most populous state in the USA, with approximately 30 million inhabitants. The population declines rapidly as one goes north. Washington and Oregon combined have approximately 10 million inhabitants.

Settlement patterns

The original 13 colonies of America were settled by religious groups fleeing persecution, such as Catholics in Maryland, Puritans in Massachusetts, Jews in Rhode Island; land speculators and other concerns with grants from the King that sold passage and land to immigrants, such as the Virginia Land Company; and criminals in the Georgia penal colony. Virtually all of the settlers to the original 13 colonies came from the British Isles, except the black slaves.

The English were followed by Irish, Germans and Scandinavians, who settled in areas such as Minnesota for Scandinavians and Pennsylvania for Germans. The Irish became the next wave of immigrants (1840–60), mostly settling in the north to work in the new industrialized states. In the south the original English settlers simply imported slaves from Africa and the West Indies. Until the 1880s the northern band of states and the territories to the west were settled by northwestern Europeans while the original 11 Confederate states and the lands to the west remained predominately Anglo-Saxon with large black populations.

Between 1880 and the 1920s, the pattern shifted to Southern and Eastern Europe. Italians, Jews, Poles and more came literally by the millions to populate northern and midwestern cities. The South's reliance on black labor retarded immigration. World War I and the Depression and then World War II limited immigration. The post-WWII immigration which grew from a trickle in the 1950s to a flood by the year 2000 included millions of Asians (with the elimination of the Asian Exclusion Act in the mid 1970s), Mexicans, Eastern Europeans with the fall of communism, other folks from Latin America, and a reduced percentage of Europeans.

A bit of history

Each of the original 13 colonies had independent relations with London. Most of the colonies claimed all of the land to the west to the Pacific Ocean. Many of the land claims conflicted and had to be resolved upon independence.

The events leading to the American Revolution started with the costs and hardships born by the colonials in the Anglo-French wars for supremacy of North America. The Seven Years War was resolved in 1763, with the French ceding most of area between the Mississippi and Appalachian Mountains to the British. The colonists felt they did most of the work, only to be subject to successively higher taxation. Furthermore, the British created an Indian reserve west of the Appalachians, making further settlement illegal. Trappers and traders, ironically predominately of French origin, followed by settlers, defied the settlement ban. This caused deteriorating relations between the American Indians, who were being pushed west, the colonists, who were pushing west, and the British, who were trying to keep a lid on things.

The American Revolution

There are always real reasons and good reasons for everything. The good reasons for the American Revolution were no taxation without representation, and protection of civil liberties from an overbearing king who couldn't even speak English. This sentiment was summed up by John Patrick Henry of the Virginia colony who proclaimed 'give me liberty or give me death'. He got liberty and wealth, so it all worked out.

The same John Patrick Henry articulated the real reason. He wrote of a commercial empire, without duties or borders, stretching from coast to coast, bound by rivers and roads. Business interests at the time understood what was at stake and declined British assistance to achieve the goal. The debate over the extent of the empire and the means of achieving it has been one of the most divisive points of American politics since revolutionary times.

A new nation

Thomas Hart Benton, a senator from Missouri during the first half of the 19th century, continuing John Patrick Henry's theme, viewed the USA as a continental power dominating Pacific trade and the new road to India. Senator Benton's protégé and son-in-law John C Fremont, whose life spanned virtually the entire 19th century, sharing a similar vision, may have done more than any single person to understand what the continent had to offer and how to tie it together. Many of our modern freeways follow routes surveyed by Fremont. For example, I70 leads to the South Pass over the Rockies; I10 follows much of the old Spanish Trail, and I 84 follows the Oregon Trail. For a fascinating account of Fremont's travels and accomplishments I recommend *Path Finder, John C Fremont and the Course of the American Empire* by Tom Chaffin.

The Treaty of Versailles of 1783 resulted in a USA that stretched from the Atlantic Ocean to the Mississippi River. The new country immediately began pushing west. The area between the Appalachians was divided into square mile sections, land grant universities formed and cities grew along the river systems. Napoleon sold the Louisiana Territory to the USA in 1803. Napoleon not only needed funding for his European conquests, I presume he figured the USA would take it if he didn't sell first. This tract included most of central North America.

Land claims

Thomas Jefferson sent Lewis and Clark to explore the new territory. Lewis and Clark surveyed the area between the Mississippi and Pacific Ocean, following the Missouri River, Snake River and Columbia River and arriving at what is now Astoria, Oregon, in 1806. Their reports of fantastic land, furs and other wealth incited further waves of western migration.

First came the trappers who had already reached the Rocky Mountains and beyond. The trappers were followed by settlers who claimed land where they stopped. There were multiple claimants to the land: the US government, Indians, British, Spanish, Russians. There was no system for recording land ownership, even if there was somebody to buy the land from. The rule of thumb was that one needed ten signatures of free white males to prove title to land for sale. Most states still require ten signatures from taxpayers to support an application to be a Notary Public. Squatters simply colonized land without paying for it. As squatter towns grew the politicians, naturally believing the US government owned the land, had the choice of ratifying the theft or calling in the army. Many of the acts granting land as an incentive to settlement were more about ratifying squatter rights than enticing new settlers.

The Indian and Mexican Wars

The Indians soon became hostile, resulting in settler deaths. The government sent survey parties to determine the best places to establish forts to protect settlers. The forts tended to increase settlement and hence increase Indian wars. The last of the Indian wars or disturbances, if you will, occurred in the very early 1900s.

The most famous surveyor, John C Fremont, whether on secret orders or not, surveyed the Indian and Spanish roads of Spanish North America, later Mexico. By the 1830s American settlement of Texas, from the Mexican point of view, reached alarming proportions. The Texans seceded from Texas, creating a new country that was annexed by the USA in 1845. This precipitated the Mexican War, resulting in the acquisition of virtually all the remainder of the continental USA except Washington, Oregon and British Columbia under joint Anglo-US control. Soon after the USA and Britain agreed to the current boundary.

Not so coincidentally, Fremont was in Mexico when the Mexican War started. He led a settlers' army against the locals, called 'Californios'. Fremont was immediately supported by US navy and army units. A review of the major streets of San Francisco, then a village called Yerba Buena, reveals the names of some of the main characters, such as Fremont – John C Fremont; Sutter – the Swiss settler who played for both sides; Stockton – a naval commander. On the Mexican side Mariano Vallejo, whose name appears on cities, streets and wine, became one of California's most illustrious citizens. Pio Pico – see Pico Boulevard in LA – became one of the organizers of Standard Oil of California.

Territorial acquisition

The addition of Florida, Alaska and Hawaii completed the current boundaries of the USA. Alaska was purchased in 1867 for $7,200,000.00, or approximately 2.5 cents per acre for 586,400 square miles of territory, twice the size of Texas. Hawaii was part of the settlement of the Spanish American War of 1898 and Florida was purchased from Spain in 1819 for $5 million.

The Mexican War was a watershed event in American politics. Prior administrations acquired land by negotiation and purchase. The Polk administration was in part elected to instigate a war with Mexico with the goal of territorial acquisition. As a result of the success of the Mexican War the USA more aggressively sought new territories. The excuse ranged from spreading Christianity to natives and more recently making the world safe for democracy. Some would say that nothing changed but the name of the religion. For example, there were failed attempts to annex Japanese islands, and British Columbia. The Spanish American War of 1898 resulted in the acquisition of Guam, Hawaii, the Philippines and Cuba. From 1783 to the present the USA went from consisting only of the Atlantic seaboard of North America to being the major world power, in many regards supplanting the British Empire, maintaining troops in Japan, Korea, Europe, Iraq and elswehere.

Since the Polk administration both major political parties have been proponents of US expansion. To the extent there is a political debate, it concerns how to spend what's left after defense spending. My humble prediction is that the next great debate in US politics, possibly resulting in the formation of a new political party, will occur when, primarily for financial reasons, the USA must retrench, or 'roll back the empire' and allow other countries to share in the maintenance of world peace.

Racial desegregation

The elimination of racial segregation in 1964–66 proved to be another watershed event. Before desegregation blacks were allocated everything from separate water fountains and bathrooms to schools and neighborhoods. It came to a point when northern and foreign companies simply couldn't expand to the South unless there was racial equality. The South's segregation laws caused the region to lag behind the North economically so that one could say parts of the South were more third world than first world. This, combined with a post-World War II generation of blacks who had fought for their country but had to live in substandard conditions, created the conditions for desegregation.

I grew up in Miami, now a cosmopolitan city, then one of the most segregated cities in the world. I traveled in the back of the bus with our black mammy, attended a segregated school and got laughed at if I was stupid enough to drink from the wrong water fountain. Segregation didn't mean that whites and blacks didn't mix. We played with our mammy's kids, played no pads sand lot football white against black and then hired the kids we grew up with to take care of the garden. As it turns out Strom Thurmond, the Dixicrat leader, had a mixed race daughter. Strom is in good company, there are a lot of mixed blood Jeffersons and Washingtons also.

Desegregation happened quickly and, despite the newsreels, in the scheme of things peacefully. Blacks and whites in the South actually knew each other and in many ways were relieved by the end of the racial barriers. In the North blacks lived in the same ghettos originally founded by the Irish, and too many remain in the same place.

By the early 1970s Northerners were moving south in droves for better climate, and northern companies, followed by foreign companies, set up shop in southern cities, seeking reasonably priced labor. The South boomed and rapidly achieved economic parity with the North.

The demographics of the 'Stars and Bars' states, Florida and Texas in particular, changed to the point where the Democratic Party, the pro-slave party during the civil war, which hadn't lost a southern election for almost any office since 1865, lost power to the Republican Party in the early 1970s. The coalition of the newly Republican southern and southwestern states created a Republican majority that lasts to this day. For those interested in this subject I recommend Kevin Phillips' *The Emerging Republican Majority 1969*, an interesting analysis of changing migration patterns and their effect on politics.

While I'm simplifying a complex situation, the salient fact is that the South made remarkable changes in a very short time. At the moment Florida is one of the favored destinations for British, German and Dutch citizens. This would never have been the case when I lived there. After the events of 9/11 the flow of immigrants slowed as the worldwide economy retracted, coupled with the insecurity of terrorism.

Immigration the capitalist way

The US immigrant investor program (EB-5) started in 1990 in response to an economic recession and to cash in on some of the success the Canadians were having at that time with their program. It requires a minimum 'at risk' investment of $500,000. The US program does not offer the certainty of result offered by Australia and Canada, who guarantee return of capital, or the opportunity simply to invest in bonds or securities as in New Zealand and the UK. The US investment must be 'at risk' (no guarantees allowed).

When to make the investment

Technically, Citizenship and Immigration Services (CIS) permits escrow or trust arrangements to hold invested funds pending visa approval. In practice, visa approval comes faster and more often if the applicant completes the investment before applying for permanent residence status. Committing to the investment before applying for the visa eliminates grounds for suspecting the bona fides of the investment scheme. Applicants for the US program should thoroughly investigate the underlying investment before applying. You may own it whether the visa is approved or not.

Evaluating an investment program

When analyzing an EB-5 program, ask yourself if you would make the investment without immigration benefits. If the answer is no, you are probably dealing with a company in business to collect fees from immigrants rather than invest immigrant capital to create wealth for its investors and jobs for the economy. You are not buying a green card. You are making an investment. The green card, a by-product of your investment, depends on your contribution to the economy – i.e., new capital and job creation. In short, one must demonstrate the viability of the business proposition to maximize the chances of visa approval.

Who is eligible

The EB-5 visa includes the applicant, spouse and dependents under 21 years of age. EB-5 visa holders may seek employment and attend school in the USA. Many EB-5 investors even become involved in charity or part-time work. Simply put, the EB-5 visa offers the opportunity to do what you want in the USA.

EB-5 visa holders do not need to directly manage a business or enterprise in the USA. A minority of EB-5 applicants manage their own business. Most applicants use the EB-5 category to obtain visa status without committing to a particular job or management responsibility. One can make further investment or employment decisions upon better understanding the pros and cons of life in the USA. Applicants should exhaust other visa options before committing to a substantial investment.

A quick checklist to determine who should NOT use the EB-5 category

- If you have a US citizen parent or child over 21 years of age, you should consider family class visa categories.

- If you have exceptional skills or are famous, you may qualify for a green card based on your skills or fame.

- If you want to manage your own business, consider L-1 and E-2 international manager visa categories.

A passive investment?

Confusion abounds concerning whether EB-5 is *a truly passive investment*. I address this issue before describing the rules and requirements because most EB-5 investors do not want to be tied to a job upon arriving in the USA. The EB-5 regulations require involvement in management or policy making. The regulations deem a limited partner in a limited partnership that conforms to the Uniform Limited Partnership Act as sufficiently engaged in an EB-5 enterprise. A corporate director would similarly qualify. While investors may utilize any form of ownership, many EB-5 investment schemes often utilize limited partnerships simply because CIS sanctions that form of ownership in its regulations.

Limited partnerships act like a partnership for tax purposes, and limit the limited partner's liability to their capital investment but prohibit limited partners from actively engaging in management. On one hand you must be involved in management or policy making, while on the other hand you can't without becoming liable for the entire enterprise. This contradiction may be resolved by granting the limited partners the right, as a group, to oust the general partner for 'cause' and to suggest or recommend issues of overall policy. This compromise seems to satisfy CIS without creating additional liabilities for limited partnership purposes.

The EB-5 program – the general rules

The fifth employment-based preference (EB-5) immigrant visa category requires a $1 million investment with ten new employees anywhere in the USA or a $500,000 investment with ten new employees in an area where the unemployment rate exceeds the national average unemployment rate by 150% (Regular Program). Investments must be 'at risk' and in an active trade or business. Real estate development qualifies. Merely purchasing a property to manage may not qualify. Investments in listed stocks or bonds, bank deposits and other purely passive investments do **not** qualify. Note that the UK, Australia, New Zealand and Canada all permit passive investments to qualify for their respective programs.

The EB-5 visa is issued on a conditional basis for two years. One must apply for removal of conditions 90 days before the end of the two-year period. The petition for removal of conditions, discussed later, requires proof that the qualified investment was maintained for two years and that the immigrant investor was responsible for hiring ten employees as of the end of the two-year period.

The Regular Program's biggest defect is that an investment of $500,000 or $1,000,000 generally will not support ten direct employees. Further, most immigrant investors are looking for quality of life and do not want to manage ten employees in a foreign country. The Regional Center program addresses this issue by permitting investors to rely on statistically verified indirect employment as opposed to simply hiring ten persons.

The key differences between the regular program and the Regional Center program are as follows. The regular program involves a direct investment into a trade or business that hires ten persons or more. The investor may be a minority partner and may or may not directly manage the enterprise.

Regional Center investments involve investing in a managed program that does not require ten direct employees, where the investor plays a limited role in management.

Regional centers

The INS (now CIS) designated specific areas or enterprises, called *Regional Centers,* as eligible to receive immigrant investor capital (Regional Center program or Pilot program). They may solicit groups of investors to pool investment capital into specified projects located within the Regional Center. These enterprise areas may be publicly or privately managed. Regional Center investors may rely on indirect job creation rather than directly hiring ten employees; this lack of direct employees makes the Regional Center program attractive. A competent professional, such as an economist, must quantify the indirect employment. If the Regional Center is located in a high unemployment area the required capital is reduced to $500,000.

There are approximately 25 approved Regional Centers, most of them inactive. Regional Center investment opportunities range from renovating industrial warehouses for lofts, offices and other mixed uses to investment in almond groves. See Appendix A for the current list.

The USA, following the footsteps of Australia and Canada, totally revised the program in 1998 to root out several abusive practices. Most commonly, promoters funded investments with promissory notes that were never paid in full. INS, now CIS, created new rules in 1998, which it applied retroactively to approved petitions. This resulted in litigation, which continues to this day. Between 1998 and the summer of 2003 CIS approved a mere handful of EB-5 visas. In the summer of 2003, INS began approving EB-5 visa petitions according to the 1998 rules. The 1998 rules came in the form of precedent case decisions rather than regulations. Until CIS issues final regulations we can only describe the type of cases that CIS now approves.

Summary of EB5 investment options

- Invest $1 million in any location and hire at least ten employees.

- Invest $500,000 in an area of high unemployment (1.5 x national unemployment average) and hire at least ten employees.

- Invest $500,000 in a rural area with 20,000 population or less and hire ten employees.

- Invest $1,000,000 or $500,000, depending on location or unemployment statistics, in a Regional Center and rather than having direct employees rely on verified indirect employment.

Those who want to directly manage their business or investment should consider options 1–3 above, while those who would rather not take on active management of an enterprise and management of employees should consider the Regional Center alternative. The major decision is between directly managing a business and the employees or trusting most management decisions to a third party and eliminating the problems inherent in managing employees.

The details – an analysis of the statutory requirements

Qualified immigrants

Outside of the investment and employment requisites, the statute does not specifically address who may be a qualified applicant. Most immigrant investor programs target persons of specific skills and experience. The US program requires no particular experience, education or proof of business acumen. Solely owned corporations may qualify, while the CIS appears to preclude multiple shareholder corporations or other non-individual investors.

A single business may accept more than one investor, provided that: (1) each petitioning investor invested the required amount; and (2) each investment results in the creation of at least ten full-time, direct or indirect, positions for qualifying employees. EB-5 investors do not have to own a minimum percentage of the enterprise. Furthermore, an investment may qualify with several owners, including persons not seeking an immigration benefit. In this case employment creation may be allocated to those seeking EB-5 classification.

A partnership with multiple partners, investing in real estate, may qualify. A venture fund that pools capital to invest in several businesses should qualify under the law but doesn't qualify under current policy. This means multiple investors may invest in one property or business, but not divide their investment among several businesses or properties.

The new commercial enterprise

The enterprise must be 'new', i.e. formed after 29 November 1990. The term 'commercial' includes any for-profit entity formed for the ongoing conduct of lawful business. Purchasing a personal residence or investing in a non-profit enterprise does not qualify. The commercial enterprise may utilize virtually any form of ownership. The petitioner may join an existing business, start a new business or restructure an existing business by increasing the net worth or number of employees in the business by 140%. In the case of a restructured business, the investor need only maintain, not expand, existing employment.

'Engaging' in a new commercial enterprise

An investor must maintain more than a purely passive role in the target investment. The regulations require an EB-5 immigrant's involvement in at least policy formulation for the new commercial enterprise. The regulations state that corporate officers or board members, or limited partners under the provisions of the Uniform Limited Partnership Act, qualify as 'engaged' in management. The requirement for something more than passive participation in management was designed to require applicants to bring managerial skills as well as capital to the USA.

'Investing' or 'actively in the process of investing' capital

The statute requires an EB-5 petitioner to have invested or be in the process of investing. The term 'invest' means to contribute capital. 'Capital' means cash and cash equivalents, equipment, inventory and other tangible property. Investors may borrow capital from third parties as long as they are personally and primarily liable for the debt. The assets of the target investment may not be used to secure any of the indebtedness. Furthermore, the investor cannot receive any sort of redemption arrangement other than those using fair market value for the buy back price. All capital is valued at fair market value in US dollars at the time of investment.

Prior to 1998, CIS permitted investors to make capital contributions in installments over time. Current policy requires a one-time cash investment. In practice, the only safe way to qualify for EB-5 is to contribute the required capital, at one time, in cash.

Benefiting the US economy

The statute requires that investments 'benefit the US economy'. The statute provides no guidance on which investments benefit the economy. Demonstrable job creation generally satisfies this requirement.

Creating or saving jobs

To qualify for EB-5 status, an investment normally must create ten full-time jobs for US citizens, lawful permanent residents or other persons lawfully authorized for employment in the United States. The investor, the investor's spouse and children, and non-immigrants do not count toward the ten-employee minimum. The 'other immigrants' provision refers to other immigrants permitted to work who also qualify as employees for EB-5 purposes.

An 'employee' for EB-5 purposes must provide services or labor and receive remuneration directly from the new commercial enterprise. This definition excludes independent contractors. Qualifying jobs must be full-time, a minimum of 35 working hours per week. Two or more qualifying employees may share a full-time position if the position requires at least 35 hours per week. Part-time positions or independent contractors do not count for direct employment under any circumstances.

The EB-5 **Regional Center** program does not require the investment to directly create ten jobs. Instead, pilot program investments only require indirect creation of jobs. Most Regional Centers hire an independent economist to document the indirect employment multiples derived from the investment activity.

When the jobs must exist

The statutory language does not require jobs to exist at the time of initial investment. One may proffer a comprehensive business plan demonstrating a need for at least ten employees within the next two years, or in the case of a Regional Center, an economist's opinion concerning indirect employment. The business plan need only indicate the approximate dates during the following two years when the employees will be hired. The temporary vacancy of a position during the two-year conditional period does not disqualify an investor who makes a good-faith attempt to re-staff the position. The jobs must exist at the time one files for removal of conditional status.

Where the jobs must be located

Congress designed the EB-5 program to create jobs in the geographic areas that need them most. The statute sets aside 5,000 of the approximately 10,000 EB-5 visas available annually for investment in 'targeted employment areas'. The statute defines a 'targeted employment area' as a rural area or an area that has experienced unemployment of at least 150% of the national average. An area outside of a metropolitan statistical area (as designated by the Office of Management and Budget) with a population of 20,000 or less is considered a rural area. Each state notifies the CIS which state agency will apply these guidelines, and determines targeted employment areas for that state.

Troubled businesses

Special rules govern investments in 'troubled' businesses. A troubled business is one that has been in existence for at least two years, has incurred a net loss for accounting purposes during the 12- or 24-month period before the petition was filed, and the loss for such period is at least equal to 20% of the business's net worth before the loss. The petitioner must show that the number of existing employees will be maintained, not necessarily increased, at no less than the pre-investment level for at least two years, rather than create ten new jobs. Congress relaxed the employment requirements to encourage investors to turn around troubled businesses. Be warned that if the troubled business does not survive for two years after the investment, the investor might lose conditional residency status.

EB-5 Procedures: Initial Evidence

The regular EB-5 program and the pilot program have similar evidentiary requirements. The distinction between the two processes is that the former requires the petitioner to submit all of the described evidence; the latter, additionally, requires the designated Regional Center to demonstrate indirect employment creation. In either case the investor files for EB-5 classification using INS Form I-526. The petition must be signed by the investor.

Evidence required under the regular program is as follows:

The new commercial enterprise

To show that an investment has been made in a new commercial enterprise, evidence must include:

- An organizational document for the new enterprise, such as articles of incorporation, partnership agreements, certificates of merger and consolidation, or partnership agreements

- A business license or authorization to transact business in a state or city

- For investments in an existing business, proof that the required amount of capital was transferred to the business after 29 November 1990

Capitalization

To show the actual commitment of the required amount of capital, evidence must include:

- Bank statements showing deposits in the US account of the enterprise

- Evidence of assets purchased for use in the enterprise

- Evidence of property transferred from abroad

- Evidence of funds invested in the enterprise in exchange for stock, *or*

- Evidence of debts secured by the investor's assets and for which the investor is personally liable

Recent rulings state that merely putting cash into the corporate account of a business does not show that the capital is 'at risk'. Based on this statement we recommend fully investing before applying so that you present proof of a completed, rather than a prospective, investment.

Legal acquisition of capital

To establish a legal source of funds, you must provide:

- Foreign business registration records

- Personal and business tax returns, or other tax returns of any kind filed anywhere in the world within the previous five years

- Documents identifying any other source of money

- Certified copies of all pending governmental, civil or criminal actions and proceedings, or any private civil actions involving money judgments against the investor within the past 15 years

Although the regulations indicate that submission of any one type of document should suffice, recent rulings require investors to submit tax returns for all of the previous five years.

Creating employment

To demonstrate that a new commercial enterprise will create at least ten full-time positions, or in the case of troubled businesses, maintain the current level of employment, you must provide:

● Photocopies of relevant tax and employment records, for ten qualifying employees, *or*

● A comprehensive business plan showing the need for no fewer than ten qualifying employees, and when the employees will be hired. The plan should include a description of the business; the business' objectives; a market analysis including names of competing businesses and their relative strengths and weaknesses; a comparison of the competition's products and pricing structures; a description of the target market and prospective customers; a description of any manufacturing or production processes, materials required and supply sources; details of any contracts executed; marketing strategy including pricing, advertising and servicing; organizational structure; and sales, cost and income projections. Specifically with respect to employment, the business plan must describe staffing requirements, job descriptions for all positions and a timetable for hiring.

Managerial capacity of the investor

The petitioner must either be involved in the day-to-day managerial control of the enterprise, or manage it through policy formulation. You must provide:

● A comprehensive job description for the investor's position

● Evidence that the petitioner is a corporate officer or on the board of directors

● If you are a limited partner, evidence that you have rights, powers and duties commensurate with those normally granted under the Uniform Limited Partnership Act (ULPA). We recommend granting the limited partner the rights to serve on management committees rendering policy advice to the general partner.

Creation of employment in a targeted employment area

To show that the new commercial enterprise has created, or will create, employment in a targeted employment area, you must provide:

- For a rural area, evidence that the new commercial enterprise is not located within any standard metropolitan statistical area, or within any city or town having a population of 20,000 or more

- For a high unemployment area, a letter from the state in which the new commercial enterprise is located, which certifies that the area has been designated as a high unemployment area.

Regional Center pilot program

An investment under the pilot program must be made in a commercial enterprise located within a Regional Center. The petition should include a copy of the letter designating the Regional Center. The job creation requirement (ten new jobs) is met by the aforementioned economist's opinion showing direct and indirect employment. Otherwise, the evidentiary requirements are similar to those for the regular program.

Removing the conditions

Approved I-526 petitioners, under either the regular or pilot program, become conditional residents for two years. Conditional residents and permanent residents without conditions have the same rights and privileges; most importantly, the ability to travel freely and work without restriction. A petition to remove the conditions (CIS form I-829) must provide evidence that a commercial enterprise was established, that the individual invested the required capital, and that the investment created ten full-time jobs, or in the case of Regional Centers, indirectly created ten full-time jobs. In substance, the investor must meet the capital investment and employment requirements and continuously maintain the investment during the two-year conditional period.

Failure to file form I-829

An immigrant investor in conditional resident status must submit form I-829 to the appropriate service center within the 90-day period immediately preceding the second anniversary of his or her admission to the United States as a conditional permanent resident. Failure to do so will result in automatic termination of the conditional resident's status and initiation of removal proceedings.

Approval of form I-829 by the INS service center

If approved, the service center director will remove the conditions on the conditional resident's status as of the second anniversary of admission as a conditional resident. The approval notice will instruct the conditional resident to report to the appropriate district office for processing for a new permanent resident card (form I-551).

Denial of form I-829 by the district director

There is no appeal against this decision. The conditional resident may seek review of the district director's decision in removal proceedings.

Case Study: American Life

Its often useful to explain complex rules and procedures by example. The following is taken from the Frequently Asked Questions page of the Americanlifeinc.com website, www.amlife.us. Many of American Life's investors qualify for EB-5 status. The company renovates warehouses in Seattle, Washington. Immigrant investors as well as investors not seeking an immigration benefit invest in a limited partnership that owns and renovates out-of-date industrial properties. The job creation comes from indirect employment derived from making the warehouses useful to a wider variety of tenants than possible before the renovation. The purpose here is to illustrate how a qualifying program may be organized; not to sell American Life. There are many fine programs, using different models, that qualify for EB-5.

While there are several Regional Centers in the application process and several approved but inactive Regional Centers, I'm aware of only four actively marketed Regional Centers. Interested parties should consult the CIS website for the latest information (www.uscis.gov).

The four actively marked Regional Centers are as follows:

- California Consortium for Agricultural Export, Spencer Enterprises. Contact Susan Spencer on email: sspencer@ccax.com.

- CCAX (www.ccax.com). The company website describes the business opportunity as: 'Funds are used to create a business that purchases 80 acres of land in Central California and grows almonds for export.'

- Philadelphia Industrial Development Corporation, CanAm Enterprises (www.canamenterprises.com). Contact Tom Rosenfeld on email: tom@canamenterprises.com. The company website describes the opportunity as: 'The City of Philadelphia's non-profit development agency, the Philadelphia Industrial Development Corporation (PIDC), and CanAm Enterprises, LLC are pleased to introduce the PIDC Regional Center, which will offer investment opportunities pursuant to the U.S. Immigrant Investor Program.' Put another way, CanAm Enterprises arranges investment opportunities for immigrant investors wishing to invest in the PIDC Regional Center. The investment opportunities range from loans to operating businesses such as restaurants to building remodels. The investment opportunities change from time to time.

- South Dakota International Business Institute, Dairy Economic Development Region (www.sd-exports.org). Contact Joop Bollen on email: bollenj@northern.edu. This is the newest Regional Center. They arrange investment in dairy farms and related businesses.

Q: How is your investment structured?

Each limited partnership owns one building. Your investment purchases an interest in the limited partnership. You become a limited partner. Your percentage share of the limited partnership depends on the percentage your investment bears to the value of the project. The prospectus for each project describes the valuation methodology.

American Life Inc is the general partner of the limited partnership. The general partner directs the property renovation, leases the property and provides general property management. The limited partners receive their share of the income from the property. Immigrant investors and investors who do not seek an immigration benefit receive 70% of the partnership profits from the time of their initial investment.

American Life investment partnerships are open to those seeking an immigration benefit and those who invest only for economic reasons on the same terms and conditions. 'Non-immigrant' investors significantly outnumber immigrant investors.

Q: What is a limited partnership?

This is best explained through an overview of the various entities available to investors.

A **corporation**, formed by filing a charter with a state government, is owned by shareholders. The corporation is taxed on its income. The shareholders are only taxed on dividends paid to them by the corporation. Shareholders do not pay tax on the corporation's income. The shareholders only risk the cost of their investment in the corporation; they bear no responsibility for the general affairs of the corporation.

A **partnership** is comprised of two or more people or entities coming together for an enterprise, without any particular state charter. The partnership does not pay tax, but passes through all items of income and loss to the partners. The partners pay tax on partnership earnings. Each partner, unlike a corporate shareholder, undertakes responsibility for the entire operations of the partnership. If the partnership were to be sued and judged liable, each partner bears full responsibility for the damages. A corporate shareholder has no such direct liability.

A **limited partnership** combines corporate limited liability with partnership taxation. The limited partnership, formed by filing a charter with a state government, consists of a general partner and one or more limited partners. The charter details the rights and powers of the limited and general partners, percentages of ownership, and distributions of profits. The general partner manages the business. As in a corporation, the limited partners are passive investors liable only for the value of their investment. As in a general partnership, limited partnership income is taxed at the partner level, not at the entity level.

A **limited liability company** is a corporation that passes through income and loss to the shareholders but offers shareholders the same limited liability as a limited partner or corporate shareholder. You could say a limited liability company is a corporate version of a limited partnership.

Q: How is my limited partner interest protected?

The Certificate of Limited Partnership must be recorded with the State of Washington as a public record. The Certificate refers to a Schedule A of the limited partnership agreement, which lists the names and percentage interests of the limited partners. The deed for the investment property is held in the name of the limited partnership. The deed is also of public record. This means the property cannot be sold, mortgaged or altered without complying with the terms of the limited partnership agreement.

Q: Is my investment guaranteed?

No. The law requires an 'at risk' investment without guarantees or redemption rights.

Q: What are my risks?

As in any investment, there is a risk of total loss. We invest in real estate without mortgage or bank financing. This lack of debt eliminates much of the risk of total loss. Like everybody, we risk the deleterious effects of acts of God, war, and market fluctuations in rental income or real estate prices. We urge all investors to visit us, check our references and to independently verify the information contained in our prospectus.

Q: Why must I invest before you will apply for my green card?

We understand that other investment companies accepting EB-5 investors place funds in a trust or escrow account pending visa approval. In this case the funds may only be released upon visa approval.

Our primary business is real estate development. Most of our capital comes from investors who do not seek an immigration benefit. These investors invest on financial consideration only, without preconditions. EB-5 investors have two considerations, the soundness of the investment and obtaining their green card. The investment must be analyzed upon its merits. If you believe we offer a sound investment, then we require that you commit your capital as any other investor.

Escrow or trust agreements present immigration difficulties. We offer investment opportunities on a first-come, first-served basis. While your investment capital sits in escrow or trust pending the results of a visa application, which may take six to eight months to complete, the target investment, which formed the basis of your visa petition, may have been sold out to other investors. You would be in the unfortunate position of basing your green card on an investment that didn't exist, and run the risk of having your application denied. Finally, although the regulations permit escrow arrangements, we find that CIS looks more favorably on petitions based on a completed investment, rather than a pending one.

Q: Many EB-5 programs include immigration processing as part of the investment package. Why doesn't American Life Inc. do the same?

We believe that it is important for you to have independent legal counsel representing your interests without conflict. American Life Inc.'s skill is in real estate investment. We believe it is better to focus on what we do best, safeguarding your investment. We will be happy to suggest an attorney. You will make your own arrangements with the attorney. American Life Inc. will endeavor to make the attorney's job as easy as possible.

Q: Where can I find a copy of the relevant law and regulations to study?

Please go to the US Citizenship and Immigrations Services website. A direct link to investment visa information is:
http://www.USCIS.gov/graphics/services/residency/investment.htm

Q: How can I verify that you are an honest and competent company?

We offer the references listed below. We also can make arrangements for you to contact existing investors.

Q: How long does CIS take to process my visa petition?

Processing times vary from as little as a few weeks to as much as six months. We can't predict or promise a particular processing time. You should plan for the entire process to take approximately one year.

Q: What are the processing procedures?

A general outline of the application process follows. Your attorney will be able to give you a more complete description.

Step 1) File form I-526 Petition for Alien Entrepreneur with the California Service Center. This petition requests CIS to certify the applicant and the investment as eligible for EB-5 visa status.

Step 2) Upon approval of the I-526 petition, (a) if you are in the United States, you may apply for Adjustment of Status to Permanent Residence by sending form I-485 and supporting documents to the CIS regional processing center nearest your US residence. (b) If you are abroad, you must wait for notification from the Embassy in your home country to prepare documents for the visa interview.

The purpose of the Adjustment of Status or consular visa interview is to make sure you are not subject to a grounds of exclusion, e.g., a criminal past, infectious diseases, etc.

Step 3) Upon approval you receive a form evidencing the approval as well as a travel document. You will also receive the temporary green card in the mail. If you are abroad, you must enter the US within six months of the date of the Embassy approval.

Step 4) After two years, you may file for removal of conditions or your permanent green card using Form I-829. This procedure permits CIS to verify that you have maintained your approved investment for the required two-year period.

Important tax considerations

The United States charges income tax on all US citizens and permanent residents based on worldwide income. Treaties and various exemptions eliminate some, but not all, of the risk of double taxation. Each state of the United States has its own tax system. All but four states raise revenue through state income tax. Investors should consider the tax effects of becoming a US resident before investing. As a general rule, if you are moving all of your assets to the USA, you will not have a problem with double taxation. If you will continue working or investing in your home country after moving to the US, a trip to your tax advisor is in order.

Conclusion

The US Immigrant Investor program offers a convenient way to obtain green cards for those willing to take the financial risk. The Regional Center program particularly suits those wishing to move to the US without being tied to employment. The US program requires an at risk investment in a trade or business. Virtually all the competing programs permit much safer investments in government obligations or listed securities. While one could argue the relative social benefits of the competing approaches, the salient fact is that the US program requires applicants to assess a business venture or investment opportunity, rather than merely calling a stockbroker or purchasing a gilt bond.

For the time being, the US authorities seem favorably disposed toward the Immigrant Investor program. The pre-1998 litigation, so far, has not impacted recent applications. To further protect investors, in the summer of 2003, the 9th Circuit Court of Appeals ruled that CIS could not apply rules retroactively to previously approved petitions. This means investors may rely on the rules at the time they invested. One would think such a ruling would be unnecessary.

The public tends to be more accepting of Immigrant Investor programs during times of high unemployment rates and weak economic growth. While the recent opening of the US program might be unrelated to economic factors, which I doubt, it looks like smooth sailing for the near future.

20 · Vanuatu

People establish permanent residency in Vanuatu for two principal reasons: tax savings and a carefree tropical lifestyle. Vanuatu offers good communications, an international banking community, easy access to Australia and New Zealand and reasonably priced modern housing.

Geography

Vanuatu is a group of islands located in the Coral Sea about 1,100 miles east of Australia. There are 12 main islands with two main towns. The largest town has a population of about 20,000. The total population is 170,000. Efate is the island Captain Cook called Sandwich, after Lord Sandwich. The islands are mountainous, some with active volcanoes. Vanuatu has direct air links to New Zealand and Australia as well as other South Pacific destinations.

History

The Spanish first arrived in the islands in 1606, and Captain Cook charted the islands in 1774. European settlement began in 1820 or so. In 1906 Britain and France established a condominium over the islands which continued until independence in 1980. Most of the population is Melanesian with small numbers of Europeans and Asians. Three languages are spoken: French, English and Bichelama, an English-based pidgin.

Vanuatu gained its independence from Britain and France in 1980. It has a parliamentary democracy with a unicameral Parliament. The constitution also provides for a National Council of Chiefs, which advises on matters of custom and land. The legal system in Vanuatu is primarily based on English common law with a lesser influence from the French system.

Economy

Vanuatu's economy is based primarily on fishing and subsistence or small-scale agriculture. The tropical, wet climate offers good growing conditions for many tropical crops, such as coconuts, bananas and coffee. Tourism is becoming the chief industry. Several international hotels and restaurants in Port Vila and Santo service the tourist and cruise ship industry. The other large industry is offshore finance. Vanuatu doesn't have a corporations tax, income tax or capital gains tax. As a result, many foreign companies and individuals establish Vanuatu domicile to avoid higher taxes at home.

Residency permits

A residency permit is required by anyone who stays in Vanuatu for longer than four months in any one year. The rules are simple. One must demonstrate a Vanuatu net worth of US$104,000 and monthly income of US$2,600. One must invest at least 5,000,000 Vanuatu dollars in a government approved investment. Fees are based on the term of the permit. The larger the investment the longer the permit.

Investment	Term	Fee
5,000,000	5 Years	130,000
50,000,000	10 Years	230,000
100,000,000	15 Years	330,000

Amounts are in Vanuatu dollars. US$1 = 140 Vanuatu.

All fees are payable in advance and are not refundable if the permit is granted. In the first year, VT$50,000 is charged while VT$20,000 is charged for each subsequent year.

The minimum investment is VT$5,000,000. Investments may be be held in either cash or assets. All assets must be certified by a recognised law firm, accounting firm or local domestic bank before being committed to an approved investment. Non-citizens who have resided continuously for 10 years in Vanuatu may apply for citizenship by naturalization.

Finally

I only know about Vanuatu from being called on by offshore banks offering trust services. The bankers who are based there seem to love the place. The word is that you get a tropical lifestyle with the comforts of home and easy escape to Australia or New Zealand when necessary.

Appendix A

Designated EB-5 Regional Centers in the United States

World Trade Center/Greenville-Spartenburg Inc.
315 Old Boiling Springs Road
Greer, SC 29650
Inactive

Beacon U.S. Studios Inc.
5610 Sanderling Way
Blaine, WA 98230
Inactive

City of New Orleans
Mayor's Economic Development Department
1300 Perdido Street, Suite 8E10
New Orleans, LA 70112
Inactive

North Country Alliance
One Lincoln Boulevard
Rouses Point, NY 12979
Inactive

Aero-Space Port International Group
512 Strander Boulevard
Tukwila, WA 98188
Active real estate development, cargo facility for regional airport

North Texas Commission
P.O. Box 610246
DFW Airport, TX 75261
Inactive

Legacy Project
1100 Spring Street, Suite 600
Atlanta, GA 30309
Inactive

Abacus Advisors, Inc.
195 Boston Post Road
Weston, MA 02193 [Now in DC]
Advertises but no apparent economic activity

American Export Partners
10 State Street
Charleston, SC 29401
Inactive

Danou Enterprises
World Trade Center Detroit/Windsor
1251 Fort Street
Trenton, MI 48183
Inactive

Pueblo Economic Development Corporation
P.O. Box 5807
Pueblo, CO 81002
Inactive

GV Development
7525 W. Highway 68
P.O. Box 10430
Golden Valley, AZ 86413–2430
Inactive

Unibex Global Corporation
1201 Eleanor Avenue
Las Vegas, NV 89106
Inactive

State of Hawaii, Department of Business, Economic
Development & Tourism
P.O. Box 2359
Honolulu, HI 96804
Actively soliciting investors to start or invest in Hawaii businesses

Atlanta International Center for Academic [sic] and Athletics
1131 Alpharetta Street
Roswell, GA 30075
Inactive

The Gateway Freedom Fund (aka Golden Rainbow Freedom Fund)
18034 13th Street
Seattle, WA 98177
*Active, real estate investment in industrial property renovation
in Seattle, Washington*

West Rand Gold Trust
P.O. Box 2222
Ridgecrest, CA 93556
Inactive

Miami Chinese Community Center, Ltd.
331 NE 18th Street
Miami, FL 33132
Inactive

CKS Western Inc. World Trade Center
620 W. Graham Drive
Lake Elsinore, CA 92530
Inactive

Empirical Entertainment

6255 Sunset Boulevard, Suite 2000

Hollywood, CA 90028

Inactive

State of Vermont Agency of Commerce and Community Development

109 State Street

Montpellier, VT 05609–0501

Active, no apparent investment activity

Trading Partners International of California LLC

2677 N. Main Street, Suite 930

Santa Ana, CA 92705

Inactive

CMB Export LLC

Corona Professional Center

400 S. Ramona Avenue, Suite 212AA

Corona, CA 91719

Inactive

Alameda Trade Center

c/o Lowe Enterprises Commercial Group

1818 East 7th Street, Suite 200

Los Angeles, CA 90021

Inactive

Matrix International, LLC

P.O. Box 22891

Seattle, WA 98122

Inactive

California Consortium for Agricultural Exports

c/o Spencer Enterprises Inc.

4974 East Clinton, Suite 200

Fresno, CA 93727

Investment in almond groves near Fresno, California, actively soliciting investors

Philadelphia Industrial Development Corporation

2600 Centre Square West

1500 Market Street

Philadelphia, PA 19102–2126

Active, inner city real estate renovations in Philadelphia

Appendix B
US Visa statistics

I-526 Petitions for Immigrant Investor Visas
By Fiscal Year 1992–2003

FY	Receipts	Approvals	Denials
1992	474	240	40
1993	436	384	170
1994	513	407	82
1995	417	291	109
1996	801	616	122
1997	1,496	1,110	141
1998	1,368	358	290
1999	650	141	1,558
2000	384	167	270
2001	585	44	207
2002	255	69	217
2003	255	132	194

Persons Granted Lawful Permanent Resident Status (Conditional)
As Investors (and their family members)
By Fiscal Year 1992–2002

FY	Total	Principals	Derivatives
1992	59	24	35
1993	583	196	387
1994	444	157	287
1995	540	174	366
1996	936	295	641
1997	1,361	444	917
1998	824	259	565
1999	286	99	187
2000	226	79	147
2001	193	67	126
2002	149	52	97
2003	NA	NA	NA

I-829 Removal of Conditional Status for Investors
By Fiscal Year 1992–2003

FY	Receipts	Approvals	Denials
1994	24	15	1
1995	130	111	10
1996	287	344	53
1997	877	718	135
1998	469	104	13
1999	384	86	24
2000	384	30	33
2001	143	52	114
2002	194	198	174
2003	139	36	66

Appendix C
Comparison of Five Major Countries

	United Kingdom	United States	Australia	Canada	New Zealand
Capital required	£1m	US$500K – $1m	US$750K – $2m	400K	US$1m
Government guarantee	no	no	yes	yes	no, unless one purchases gov guaranteed bond
Finance available	yes, HSBC	investors may borrow their investment capital	no	yes	no
Invest in publicly traded securities	yes	no	no	no	yes
Invest in active trade or business	yes	yes	no	no	yes
Required holding period	4 years	2 years	4 years	5 years	2 years
Required number of employees	none	10 direct or indirect	none	none	none
Active management required	none	yes, with some exceptions for directors and limited partners	none	none	none

Appendix D
Facts in Brief

Country	Population (2004)	Pop Growth (2004)	Currency	GDP PP Parity	GDP Growth	GDP/ Head	Social Security?	Languages	Ethnic Makeup	Climate
Belize	272,945	2.39%	Belizean dollar (BZD)	1.28 billion	3.70%	$4,900	N/A	English (official), Spanish, Mayan, Garifuna (Carib), Creole	mestizo 48.7%, Creole 24.9%, Maya 10.6%, Garifuna 6.1%, other 9.7%	tropical; very hot and humid; rainy season (May-Nov.); dry season (Feb.-May)
Bermuda	64,935	0.68%	Bermudian dollar (BMD)	2.33 billion	2%	$36,000	N/A	English (official), Portuguese	black 58%, white 36%, other 6%	subtropical; mild, humid; gales, strong winds common in winter
Italy	58,057,477	0.09%	euro (EUR)	1.55 trillion	0.40%	$26,700	Old Age, Disability, Death	Italian (official), German (parts of Trentino-Alto Adige region are predominantly German speaking), French (small French-speaking minority in Valle d'Aosta region), Slovene (Slovene-speaking minority in the Trieste-Gorizia area)	Italian (includes small clusters of German-, French-, and Slovene-Italians in the north and Albanian-Italians & Greek Italians in the south	predominantly Mediterranean; Alpine in far north; hot, dry in south
Malayasia	23,522,482	1.83%	ringgit (MYR)	207.8 billion	5.20%	$9,000	N/A	Bahasa Melayu (official), English, Chinese dialects (Cantonese, Mandarin, Hokkien, Hakka, Hainan, Foochow), Tamil, Telugu, Malayalam, Panjabi, Thai; note, in addition, in East Malaysia several indigenous languages are spoken, the largest are Iban and Kadazan	Malay and other indigenous 58%, Chinese 24% Indian 8%, other 10% (2000)	tropical; annual southwest (April-Oct.) and northeast (Oct.-Feb.) monsoons

Country	Population (2004)	Pop Growth (2004)	Currency	GDP PP Parity	GDP Growth	GDP/ Head	Social Security?	Languages	Ethnic Makeup	Climate
Malta	396,851	0.42%	Maltese lira (MTL)	7.082 billion	0.80%	$17,700	Old Age, Disability, Survivors	Maltese (official), English (official)	Maltese (descendants of ancient Carthaginians and Phoenicians, with strong elements of Italian and other Mediterranean stock)	Mediterranean with mild, rainy winters and hot, dry summers
Mexico	104,959,594	1.18%	Mexican peso (MXN)	941.2 billion	1.30%	$9,000		Spanish, various Mayan, Nahuatl, and other regional indigenous languages	mestizo (Amerindian-Spanish) 60%, Amerindian or predominantly Amerindian 30%, white 9%, other 1%	varies from tropical to desert
New Zealand	3,993,817	1.05%	New Zealand dollar (NZD)	85.34 billion	3.50%	$21,600	Old Age, Disability, and Survivors	English (official), Maori (official)	New Zealand European 74%, Maori 9.7%, other European 4.6%, Pacific Islander 3.8%, Asian and others 7.4%	temperate with sharp regional contrasts
South Africa	42,718,530	-0.25%	rand (ZAR)	456.7 billion	1.90%	$10,700	Old Age, Disability, and Survivors	11 official languages, including Afrikaans, English, Ndebele, Pedi, Sotho, Swazi, Tsonga, Tswana, Venda, Xhosa, Zulu	black 75.2%, white 13.6%, Colored 8.6%, Indian 2.6%	mostly semiarid, subtropical along east coast; sunny days, cool nights
Spain	40,280,780	0.16%	euro (EUR)	885.5 billion	2.40%	$22,000	Old Age, Disability, and Survivors	Castilian Spanish 74%, Catalan 17%, Galician 7%, Basque 2%	composite of Mediterranean and Nordic types	temperate; clear, hot summers in interior, more moderate and cloudy along coast; cloudy, cold winters in interior, partly cloudy and cool along coast
Switzerland	7,450,867	0.54%	Swiss franc (CHF)	239.3 billion	-0.50%	$32,700	Old Age, Disability, and Survivors	German (official) 63.7%, French (official) 19.2%, Italian (official) 7.6%, Romansch (official) 0.6%, other 8.9%	German 65%, French 18%, Italian 10%, Romansch 1%, other 6%	temperate, but varies with altitude; cold, cloudy, rainy/snowy winters; cool to warm, cloudy, humid summers with occasional showers

Country	Population (2004)	Pop Growth (2004)	Currency	GDP PP Parity	GDP Growth	GDP/ Head	Social Security?	Languages	Ethnic Makeup	Climate
Thailand	64,865,523	0.91%	baht (THB)	477.5 billion	6.70%	$7,400	Old Age, Disability, and Survivors	Thai, English (secondary language of the elite), ethnic and regional dialects	Thai 75%, Chinese 14%, other 11%	tropical; rainy, warm, cloudy southwest monsoon (mid-May to Sept.); dry, cool northeast monsoon (Nov–mid March); southern isthmus always hot and humid
United Kingdom	60,270,708	0.29%	British pound (GBP)	1.666 trillion	2.20%	$27,700	Old Age, Disability, and Survivors	English, Welsh (about 26% of the population of Wales), Scottish form of Gaelic (about 60,000 in Scotland)	English 81.5%, Scottish 9.6%, Irish 2.4%, Welsh 1.9%, Ulster 1.8%, West Indian, Indian, Pakistani, and other 2.8%	temperate; moderated by prevailing southwest winds over the North Atlantic Current; more than one-half of the days are overcast
United States	293,027,571	0.92%	US dollar (USD)	10.99 trillion	3.10%	$37,800	Old Age, Disability, and Survivors	English, Spanish (spoken by a sizeable minority)	white 77.1%, black 12.9%, Asian 4.2%, Amerindian and Alaska native 1.5%, native Hawaiian and other Pacific islander 0.3%, other 4% (2000)	mostly temperate, but tropical in Hawaii and Florida, arctic in Alaska, semiarid in the great plains west of the Mississippi River, and arid in the Great Basin of the southwest; low winter temperatures in the northwest are ameliorated occasionally in January and February by warm chinook winds from the eastern slopes of the Rocky Mountains
Vanuatu	202,609	1.57%	vatu (VUV)	563 million	-0.30%	$2,900	Old Age, Disability, and Survivors	three different languages: English, French, pidgin (know as Bislama or Bichelama), plus more than 100 local languages	indigenous Melanesian 98%, French, Vietnamese, Chinese, other Pacific Islanders	